MW01679732

Sales Tales

Laughs at Your Expense

by T. Farmer

DORRANCE
PUBLISHING CO
EST. 1920
PITTSBURGH, PENNSYLVANIA 15238

The contents of this work, including, but not limited to, the accuracy of events, people, and places depicted; opinions expressed; permission to use previously published materials included; and any advice given or actions advocated are solely the responsibility of the author, who assumes all liability for said work and indemnifies the publisher against any claims stemming from publication of the work.

Dorrance Publishing Co
585 Alpha Drive
Pittsburgh, PA 15238
Visit our website at www.dorrancebookstore.com

ISBN: 978-1-4809-5605-6
eISBN: 978-1-4809-5582-0

Introduction

When I think back on the many different sales jobs I have had in my life, I am not really sure how or why I pursued a sales career. College was not too appealing at first because it was four years of life with a question mark at the end. However, I do now recommend college or some higher level of education for all high school graduates. After high school my brother-in-law offered me a plumber's apprenticeship job, and I knew that if I became a journeyman plumber, I could always have a reasonably paying job for a long time. So, I served my four years of apprenticeship abuse, and after the grind was over, I joined the Army. Out of the fire and into the frying pan.

Thinking I was going to be a plumber in the Army, my plan was to use the Army education benefits to get my college education while working a normal construction routine. I must admit, when they pinned an 82nd Airborne patch on my shoulder, I was a little surprised. Boy, that recruiter was a good salesman! Even though being an airborne combat heavy engineer was very entertaining, it was not going to be a very marketable skill in the civilian world. Not too many people have jobs for someone who shoots people and blows things up. I must admit, though, I learned to love C-4, Claymore mines, and Bangalore torpedoes but, the food wasn't very good.

During the evenings, I did manage to pick up an associate degree in only thirteen months from the local university. I then applied and was accepted to an army engineer school. During my last years of military service, I was a licensed power engineer who specialized in electronic instrumentation. This education and experience was what I took into my new civilian career of selling roofing services. Yep, a licensed engineer who could operate multi-megawatt power plants and troubleshoot electronics down to component level became a roofing salesperson.

The reason I went into sales instead of engineering was that I knew someone who was making twice what I was making in the Army by knocking on some doors and talking about roofs. I thought back on my sales jobs as a youth and thought I could sell anything if I really wanted to try. No offense intended, but engineers seemed to be locked in an office or next to a desk with little chance of getting out into daylight. Sales seemed to be a low-risk option, so why not give it try? I had many sales experiences from my youth that I could possibly use to help me in this new endeavor. In a few months, I would know if I could make it work. If not, I would just go back into engineering.

When I started my sales career, I tried to reflect on any previous sales experiences I had or could remember. In my hometown of three thousand or so people, our high school was very small. My senior graduating class had about sixty-six students. I think some of my best sales pitches were given to the elementary principals. We pitched to a few teachers too. Our art teacher was somehow "sold" on us tying him up in a chair and putting a dunce hat on his head. The "sales pitch" was we were going to take a photo for the school's yearbook. He didn't know one of us had a lighter in our pocket, ready to set the paper dunce hat on fire. He freaked out of course, but the photo didn't come out very well due to the extra light from the fire on his head. Boy, did we laugh as he struggled to get himself free.

I remember one family who had a couple of children who were creative salespeople. That family owned the local Sno-Creme drive-in.

They had a son who would sell hits of acid with your burger if you let him know before ordering. Apparently, you first went by the back window, knocked on it, gave the cook a "thumbs up", then passed him a couple bucks through the window. You then had to ask for the burger to come with a slice of tomato. Now, that wasn't my idea of a good burger, but you gotta love the late '60's and early '70's! Lots of sales careers were started selling the social ills of society. I knew some very good salespeople when I was in high school. Did you?

One upperclassman named John, sold the school principal on the idea of letting his senior class barbecue a whole hog in the front yard of the high school for homecoming. He convinced the school to let him have two hundred dollars of the homecoming funds to go buy the hog and then cook it on school property. John gladly took the money, grabbed a baseball bat, and went to a local farm. Using an apple, he enticed some hogs to come over to the fence line, smashed the biggest one in the head with the bat, killing it, and he then kept the money for the after-homecoming kegger.

The school let him also buy a case of beer to baste and inject into the hog while roasting it on school property. I came across this story when I saw John sitting in a lawn chair next to a barbecue pit in the front yard of the high school, roasting the ill-gotten hog. Guess what? Not all the beer was going into the hog. John was rather inebriated that afternoon. I must admit, though, the hog tasted pretty good that night after the football game. I am not sure that kind of activity could happen at a high school today. You would have to be a great salesperson!

Most good salespeople treat every day like it is a sporting event. Many listen to motivating music before going to an appointment, just like professional athletes do when arriving at their game. Salespeople, like professional athletes, know that if you do not perform well, you in essence will lose that day. Not making a sale often means you earn little to nothing that day. You could have no money to pay your bills, or you may even be fired from your job for not meeting expectations. There is pressure to perform in order to sell and keep the engineer busy.

This demand to perform on a regular basis is why some—not all, but some—salespeople use high pressure sales tactics. Some may even lie, steal, or cheat in order to make a sale. I actually wrote an article for a trade magazine centered around the topic of why salespeople lie. Most of the time, salespeople fabricate features and benefits because they are taught these lies from their employer. Once they learn they are selling lies, they either quit or start making up some of their own. And can they make up some doozies!

I recall some window salespeople in California who worked for me coming up with Category-5 mold that causes congestive heart failure. They told homeowners it will even kill their pets. The point was to scare people to death if they had condensation or mold on the interior of their windows. To solidify this fabrication, they would reference a famous person who lost a dog due to the mold being present in their home. I tried to put an end to that story.

Despite the risky side of the sales profession, many people do take a chance to enter the sales world because it is one of the highest paying employment categories in the world. I know many salespeople who make as much or more than most lawyers and doctors. Unfortunately, for many people entering the sales profession, they fail rather quickly. Within their first few months, most new sales representatives (reps) will realize it isn't for them. For those reps who figure it out, though, they could be on the road to a magnificent and fascinating life.

To be successful in the industry, you must possess the skills of many other career fields. It is best if you have most of these skills and attitudes before you get started. If you do not have them, they can be learned with effort. Some of these skills are the reasoning and negotiation skills of a lawyer, the diagnosis and hopefully (good) bedside manners of the doctor, the analytical and process comprehension of the engineer, the math and analytical skills of an accountant, and the physical endurance of an athlete. Some of the athletic traits also include competitiveness and a short memory with regards to your failures. Let's not forget, we sometimes need psychiatric skills to help some people cope with the current crisis in their life. The personal information people share with us is often quite riveting.

Everyone, regardless of his profession, sells nearly every day of his life. If someone didn't sell what your company makes, does, or provides, you would not have a job. Teachers sell their students on their curriculum. Parents sell their children ideas and beliefs. Doctors sell patients on what they should do to get healthier. The list is endless. Sales is simply the ability to persuade and influence another person. If you want to get married, for example, you probably need to have some sales skills.

Everyone sells, but few get to enjoy the untold benefits of the sale process. The better you can sell, no matter what your profession is, the more money you can make. In my current industry, home improvement, many salespeople make anywhere from sixty thousand dollars to well over two hundred thousand dollars per year. Having sales experience with government, corporations, business-to-business, and residential sales, I have concluded that the most fun sales profession is in the residential home improvement industry. We get to see the life of the everyday American up front and in person.

In-home salespeople can make a great living, and on top of that, they get to see what really goes on inside the average American home. Considering how many different sales industries there are, few have the privilege of seeing how the everyday American lives. This world is a crazy place, and we get to see the craziest side of America every day. I think people from this industry would make great politicians because they really have seen what all Americans go through on a day-to-day basis.

You were probably taught that you cannot judge a book by its cover. However, I am sharing with you that you can judge a book by its cover. This book is not another sales training book or a mystery novel, but it is a book of sales tales. It is a compilation of weird, funny, and simply unusual stories that will hopefully give you a few good laughs.

These tales may help you get a better understanding of why some people work in the wonderful world of sales. On the other hand, it could scare you from ever considering such a line of work. There are, of course, a few underlying sales lessons, but they are not the intention of the book. I really want you to know why some of us love our profession.

Some of the tales in this book are so bizarre and so weird that we could possibly put them into some type of reality show. If you want something fun to read, this book is for you. It is a compilation of decades of funny and amazing stories that are sometimes hard to believe, but one thing is for sure: All of the stories were shared directly with me by those involved or I was part of them myself. In some of the stories, we have changed the names of those involved to protect the participants from being embarrassed. However, they are not innocent. If I have remembered or recorded any situations differently than reality, I apologize to my sales colleagues. I know they are as close as second-hand storytelling can be, though.

The first part of any good sales presentation is what we call the "warm-up." Over the years, I learned that the warm-up is still probably the most important step of any sales process. It does not matter if it is a residential, commercial, business-to-business, or government sale; the first twenty minutes of any initial contact is critical. Part of this step is to hopefully put the customer at ease and see if we can establish a level of mutual trust. This sales step is often when most nonverbal communication is misinterpreted, so we train sales reps to look clean and sharp, smile, and be neutral with their opinions. You can only give one first impression.

I often start a sales visit with an introduction of myself. At times, I will share a short story about my family name that usually comes across as somewhat humorous because it is so "country" and farmland basic. After introducing myself, I would say, "It is easy to remember my name because it is quite simple. My last name is Farmer, and I am from Iowa, which is pretty much all farmland. So, I am Farmer Tom. I have a brother named John, so we have Farmer John, and I have a brother named Jerry, so that gives you the Tom and Jerry show.

"My mom's maiden name was Akers. So, a Farmer married an Akers in Iowa. I have cousins with the last names of Gardner, Bean, and Robbins. My oldest son married a Weed, which is different because most farmers do not like weeds. My next oldest son married a Brown, so that gives us Farmer Brown. For a period of time after I got out of the military, we lived across the street from the Hays. We then bought a house and moved three blocks to be next to the Rice's. To top this all off, my Grandma Akers' dad was her uncle. By the way, the Akers clan was from Oklahoma, if that helps you understand how that could happen."

This short story about my family tree, shared during the warm-up, would normally cause the potential customer to smile and laugh. With a smile under the belt, we were ready to move on with the sales process. Humor has always been a key to most of my sales career. As a sales manager, I would often call or visit with a sales rep after his appointment. When the rep had made a sale, the most common detail shared with me regarding the new customer was that they were "really nice and a lot of fun." Interesting how that is so common.

The following stories are for kicks and giggles. Enjoy them, and remember, they are based on true events that were shared with me or they were something that happened to me personally. I hope my notes and recollections are fairly accurate. These are the reasons that many of us love our sales profession and are willing to risk the ups and downs that come along. Remember the old saying, “When you find something you love to do, you will never work a day in your life.” I haven’t worked in years!

The First Hard Lemonade Sale

Back in the late 1960's and early 1970's, it was common for our youth to start earning money by delivering newspapers, shoveling snow during winter, mowing yards in the summer, and selling refreshments at the weekend fast-pitch softball games. Looking for lost coins under the bleachers after a ball game or collecting soda pop bottles was productive too. We used to get ten cents a bottle! For the most part, we would do anything to earn money, and often it was centered around selling a product or selling our services.

One nice summer afternoon, two young boys named Tom and Bob, wearing blue jeans, white t-shirts, and Converse tennis shoes, decided to venture into a temporary job of setting up a lemonade stand in front of Bob's house. The goal of this sales endeavor was to earn enough money in a couple hours so they could buy a bottle of Orange Crush, a Topps baseball card, or Bazooka bubble gum. By the way, Tom still has his 1967 Willie Mays baseball card. Interesting what ten cents can turn into over time.

The front yard of Bob's house seemed like a good location because it was on the "other" main road into town. It was not as busy as the street where Tom lived but a busy one nonetheless. They thought more traffic would normally mean more sales, right? Well, with the goal defined and a plan at hand, the two boys set up a table in front of Bob's house and patiently began waiting for their first customer to stop. They were so excited about all the money they were going to make that day. Enthusiasm and expectations were high! There were lots of cars going down the road, so it was looking promising.

Considering the old business adage, location, location, location, the boys thought they had selected a great one, but for some reason, nobody was stopping at their stand. What they learned was that you do not set up a lemonade stand on a street where people do not stop or slow down. The traffic speed was around thirty to thirty-five miles per hour with no stop signs.

There were no local businesses close by to help slow traffic down. They had no signs nailed onto any trees a block in advance to give notice. The cars had no idea they could buy some ice cold (or lukewarm) lemonade. There were no parking areas on the street either. In fact, you could not legally stop or park on the street. Not a good choice. But, hey, they were young.

With all things considered, there was really no reason why any driver would slow down to buy some lemonade from the poor children. The cars that came by were going too fast and probably didn't even see the lemonade stand until they were almost past the boys. With little success, Tom was getting very frustrated and decided to "persuade" the traffic to stop with some "hard" sales tactics. Remember what I said earlier: Desperate salespeople sometimes use high pressure sales tactics. Tom was getting frustrated and decided somebody was going to buy lemonade, one way or the other, so he came up with a plan.

His dream of an ice-cold Orange Crush was big enough to overcome the challenge and adapt some new tactics that would lead him to success. There is a sales training quote that goes, "When the dream is big enough, the facts don't count." The boys had never heard of this saying, but it sure applied to them that day.

Tom's brilliant plan was one of those that should not be attempted at home. Do not share this with children! I do not think you will find this technique in any sales training book, even though some cold-hearted sales managers may wish their sales team was this determined.

Here is what happened. Tom knew he had to stop or slow the traffic down, so he went out into the street and laid down on his back in the path of the oncoming traffic. He put his life on the line for ten cents' worth of Orange Crush and some bubble gum. Not too smart! Sure enough, a car soon came down the street and fortunately squealed to a stop just before running over Tom.

The driver of the car was an older man. He was a middle-aged man who had one of those serious-looking faces. You know, the kind of person a younger person may have trouble trying to sell. He got out of the car shouting, "Hey! Are you all right, kid?" He had honestly thought Tom was hurt. Immediately after the man asked Tom if he was okay, Tom jumped to his feet and said enthusiastically, "Yeah, I'm okay. I just wanted you to stop and buy some lemonade!"

Now, if this had been Tom's dad, the threatened butt spanking would have actually occurred, but since he was not a relative, he merely chewed Tom out and called him the dumbest person he had ever met. There were a few other vulgarities in there, but we will keep this clean.

After the man's tirade was over, he thought about Tom's sales pitch and actually bought some lemonade! He said anyone who is stupid enough to lay down in the street to sell lemonade should at least make a sale. Tom was learning the art of persuasion and how to become a true salesperson. The ironic part of this story is that Tom was hit by a truck in Mexico as an adult. I mean, he flew off the windshield into the air and was really messed up. He did live, but he always wondered if there was some type of karma thing relevant to the lemonade incident as a kid.

Bad Monkey

There is a certain nationally-recognized cutlery company that has a reputation for making a very sharp knife. These knives are normally sold via the in-home sales process or at an event like a flea market or home show. Their sales reps sometimes go door to door trying to get into someone's home to give a demonstration. The preferred method of selling these sharp knives is by referral, of course. After you had an in-home presentation and bought a set of knives, you were offered a free knife if you provided some referrals—with phone numbers.

Such was the case when a nice lady invited the salesperson into her home. A friend had told her how great these knives were and had strongly suggested she check them out for herself. Her friend also said that the presentation was absolutely fascinating!

So, the referral call is made, a visit to the home scheduled, and then the fun begins. First, the sales rep goes to the home and knocks on the door. The lady of the home answers the door and invites the rep, Bill, into her home. As soon as he goes into the home, a small monkey comes running across the room, screaming and lunging towards him. Bill, of course, is quite startled and quickly steps back, trying to avoid the small devil. The homeowner immediately grabs the monkey and apologizes for his behavior. Behavior? The animal attacked him! Good thing the monkey did not have one of the rep's sharp knives in its hand.

The monkey was her pet, and she thought he was secured in a bedroom, but apparently, he got out. So, she takes the monkey and puts him back into his room. Afterward, she comes back out and sits with Bill at the kitchen table to start the demonstration. She was quite apologetic and said she was excited to learn about the rep's knives. By the way, how many people do you know who have a pet monkey?

After this unusual introduction, the two sat down at the kitchen table and Bill started with his warm-up, which was of course centered around her exotic pet. She shared how much she loved her pet and how she felt a connection to him. After a great warm-up, which included a laugh or two regarding the monkey, Bill goes through the demonstration showing the complete knife set. After slicing and dicing his way into her heart, he finally gets to the last knife, called the Jason knife. They refer to this big-bladed knife as the Jason knife because it looks like the one used by a character in a horror movie. Needless to say, this was a very sharp, big knife.

This was the well-rehearsed conclusion of the demonstration, and it was going to be awesome. Bill was on the verge of making a sale, and he could sense it happening. The presentation was going great! For this final portion of the presentation, some type of vegetable would be diced and sliced to perfection. The homeowner would be amazed and naturally want to buy the complete set. Well, during the Jason knife demonstration, Bill had the knife in his right hand, preparing to cut a vegetable to perfection, when all of a sudden, the monkey comes back into the room and jumps on his back, screaming and clawing at him. Bill is totally freaked out and quickly turns to swipe the monkey off his back with his right arm.

Unfortunately, Bill forgets he has the Jason knife in his hand, and while swinging at the monkey in self-defense, he cuts the monkey's head clean off. We are talking drop dead, on the spot, head chopping. The Highlander could not have done it cleaner. Absolute chaos commenced, with the homeowner crying and cursing at Bill. Blood was spewing out from the monkey's corpse as it pulsated on the floor. Wow! What a perfect, clean cut! It was a great demonstration on just how sharp the knives really were. For some reason, though, the homeowner did not buy the knife set.

It was an unfortunate accident, but it cost the knife company about $350 to buy a new monkey. Can we say, "Bad monkey?"

Abusive Mother

A strange story was shared by Dave, a replacement window sales rep who was on an appointment one evening, presenting to a nice couple of homeowners. Now, one of the goals of a good salesperson is to get the potential customers emotionally involved with the presentation. Dave was doing his normal great presentation and found he had connected emotionally with the wife. She was really getting into his presentation.

This nice mother was asking questions and being quite sincere with her involvement. Now, some people are known to have an expressive personality. One characteristic of such a person is that they talk with their hands. You know the type. When they are on the telephone, they use their hands to help the person on the other end of the line better understand the point they are trying to make.

Well, this nice mother did not notice that her young daughter, about seven years-old, had come into the room and was standing next to her. The daughter probably heard her mother getting excited about something and had to come see for herself what all the commotion was about.

With the mother caught up in the sales presentation, Dave continued with his presentation and shared an apparently exciting feature about the window. The mother was so fascinated with what she had learned, she had to use her hands to express herself. With a quick back movement of her arm and hand, the mother backhanded her young daughter in the mouth, laying her out on the floor. The young girl's mouth began to bleed, cries of pain were being declared, and chaos occurred.

The quiet father was flabbergasted to the point that he started cursing his wife. The wife became quite frantic at the sight of blood, and the daughter was looking dazed, with tears streaming down her face. Dave was sitting there watching all this commotion and thinking, "What are the odds that this could happen?"

There wasn't much he could do but sit back and let the parents figure it out. Eventually the parents realized the blood was not a major injury, and the young girl started to calm down. The funny thing is the sales rep kept his cool, let things calm down, and continued his discussion. Believe it or not, he sold the windows to the homeowners and left the home smiling. He had excellent bedside manners and a good job of keeping cool under pressure. Dave had won the game that day.

Lessons Learned from Climbing on Roofs

In the town of Woodland, California there is a nice neighborhood where many of the town's leaders live. These homes, with big roofs, are ideal for a roofing salesperson. It takes the same technique and effort once you are in a home to sell a big roofing project as it does a small one, so you might as well work where the commissions will be larger. The one challenge with the big home is the time it takes to measure and determine the homeowner's needs. Bigger roofs and bigger sales typically take more time to measure and inspect.

This particular appointment was set up with the husband, and the sales rep, Tom, did not meet the wife. He was under the impression from the husband that nobody would be home. Tom went to the home, put his ladder up on the front corner of the roof, and proceeded to inspect the roof.

After a few minutes, he decided to sit down on the roof and take a rest in the shade provided by the many trees. It was a beautiful summer day in northern California, not too hot, with a slight breeze. While sitting on the roof, he hears the front door of the home open and a man and a woman come out together. There is some small talk, and while parting, he gives her a long, passionate kiss, then gets in his car to leave.

At first, Tom thought that was cute, but then he realized that the man who left wasn't the husband who had set the appointment. Was he on the wrong roof? This is always a major concern of roofing contractors, having torn the wrong roof off before. This could be quite embarrassing if someone were to see Tom up on the wrong roof, so he did not move or make a sound. Fortunately, neither of them noticed Tom's ladder was leaning against the roof over to their left.

Tom had set the appointment with the actual husband and owner of the home, and that man was not him! What do you do? One thing for sure: Tom was not stupid enough to move around and be noticed. He sat quietly and waited for him to leave and for her to go inside. Tom also knew not to stir the pot by knocking on the door and asking her if this was the right home. He waited a few minutes, then quietly came down off the roof, took his ladder, and left the home.

Who knows, maybe they knew Tom was on the roof but didn't care. It was California, you know. Things are different there. The next day, Tom met with the husband to present his proposal. He knew not to ask the owner who the man was at the home the previous day, but he did learn the woman was his wife. Fortunately, Tom made the sale but was still very curious who the man was kissing the owner's wife.

Later that year, Tom learned that the homeowners got divorced because the husband found out she was having an affair. In small country towns, everyone learns about everyone's business. The wife moved out and didn't get the house for some reason. The husband kept the house and became a great resource for Tom, due to his leadership position in the community.

Tom could attribute over twenty sales to that homeowner because he owned multiple rental properties, and all his neighbors needed roof work too. Lesson learned: Keep your mouth shut when learning about people's business. Oh, by the way, rooftops are great places to see what goes on around a neighborhood because people do not look up.

More From Above

The roofing industry has many stories to tell and lessons to share. You could have an all-day class on the do's and don'ts of working on roofs. For example, do not tear off the wrong roof. People are a little shocked to come home and see the roof is not there. Do not step in the wrong place and fall through the attic into the living room while the retired widow is watching television.

For Tom, another lesson unfortunately occurred the same year as the previous story. He tried to apply what he had learned from the Woodland roof inspection on his next few appointments. Tom made sure the homeowner who set the appointment let their spouse or significant other know when the appointment was going to be. He also knocked on the door before going on the roof. These were two new procedures he would use going forward.

On another beautiful sunny day in California, Tom went through his new protocol. He knocked on the front door, but nobody came to the door, so he went up on the roof to begin his inspection. While inspecting the roof, he passed by a second-story window that had no curtains or blinds pulled shut to prevent someone from looking inside, so naturally, Tom looked.

Of course, as Tom walked by the window, there was a teenage girl in her bedroom changing clothes—with the curtains open!

Screams occurred from both inside and outside the home. Tom tried to move as quickly as he could on the steeper than normal roof but slipped onto his butt. The daughter could be heard screaming through the house as she ran out of her room to the nearest phone to call her parents.

Fortunately, the police were not called, but Tom had a hard time trying to explain to the mother what had happened. Apparently, when he rang the doorbell before going on the roof, the daughter did not hear it because she was playing her music. Apologies were made and skin tones returned to normal, but no sale was made that day. People do not usually buy when they are embarrassed or think you were peeping at their teenage daughter. The new lesson learned that day was to always assume someone is home and ask if they have any children who might be home.

Now, these roof inspection lessons just keep coming. One thing that is hard to teach is experience. It is true that you can share experiences, but the hands-on experience solidifies the lessons in the mind. With another roof inspection lesson learned, Tom felt he had seen it all by now. Little did he know.

A similar challenge occurred for Tom when he knocked on another door of a home that was scheduled for a roof inspection. This time, Tom made sure to knock and ring the doorbell. He had asked the husband to let his wife know he was going to be there, and he also asked if any children might be home. The husband said his son would be home, so Tom made note. He was learning!

Knowing that a teenage son would be home, Tom stayed at the front door until he answered. Seeing that he was going up on a split-level roof with an upstairs window, Tom asked if anyone was upstairs. The son said nobody was upstairs or in the home but himself. So, feeling that he had done everything he could to prevent another "peeping Tom" challenge, he proceeded up onto the roof to begin his inspection.

After looking at the front side of the home, he walked to the top of the roof and started to go on to the back side of the house. As he went over the top ridge line, he saw a beautiful pool and thought about how he wished he had a pool to use when at home. It was a beautiful pool. After coming out of his trance, Tom quickly noticed there were two women lying on lounge chairs "catching a few rays," as they say in Cali. As you may know, some women like to catch a few rays with the backs of their swimming suit untied. Tan lines are so unwelcome.

Well, when these women heard a strange, startling noise, they quickly sat up to look and had apparently forgotten that they had untied their tops. At this point, you know, the show had started!

Fortunately for Tom, when they heard the noise he made while on the roof, they didn't look up. Remember the old saying from the previous lesson, people never look up. Now, you could say fortunately they didn't look up, but some men may disagree. Immediately, Tom froze in his current position and then quietly stepped back down the other side of the roof, and the women never knew they had been peeped upon by Tom. That was close, and another lesson learned: Ask if anyone is outside sunbathing!

As a side note, one day Tom was walking around a house with the homeowner, looking up at the roof, when he accidentally stepped back into the pool. The homeowner laughed, and Tom was very embarrassed, but Tom had this one covered. As all good salespeople know, you should have a second set of clothes with you at all times, which Tom did. He went to his car, changed his clothes, and went back to his inspection.

The homeowner was so impressed by Tom's preparedness that he went ahead and bought the roofing service. We must be prepared, just like a boy scout.

Who's In the Bathroom?

One of the more important things to know as a traveling salesperson is where the clean bathrooms and good restaurants are located in your territory. Your income depends on this information. If you cannot find good food, you may find yourself having serious intestinal challenges during a presentation. If you cannot freshen up prior to an appointment, you won't feel like you have your A game going for you. This was so important to our sales team that we kept notes and shared our favorite watering holes with each other.

Hotels are known for usually having decent bathrooms on the first floor, just off the main lobby. On occasion, they will also have a decent dining establishment too. If you ever lose a phone charger, you can go to a hotel's front desk and ask if anyone has turned in a charger. They keep a box full of electronics in their lost and found and seem proud to show you their collection. They are willing to give you any part of it, too, without asking questions.

On one nice sunny afternoon, Tom was using such a bathroom off Highway-99 in California. There was only one stall in this barn, so Tom was sitting there taking care of business, and by coincidence, in walks his friend and coworker Steve.

Steve was a sales representative who worked out of the same Sacramento office as Tom. Their territory covered a 150 to 300 mile radius around Sacratomato, as we sometimes called it, since there were a lot of tomato farms around Sacramento. The chances that the two of them would be in the same area at the same time and stopping at the same bathroom had to be extremely slim. It so happened that Steve wanted—or should I say needed— to use the same, one and only stall in the bathroom that Tom was using.

Since Tom could see out easier than Steve could see in, he had the advantage for this potentially humorous moment. Steve walks over to the door, tries to open it, and notices it was locked. Tom states in a different than normal voice that this stall was currently being used and to give him a minute or two. Steve desperately asks if it would be long, and Tom mentions again, "No, just a couple minutes." Now Steve turns and walks out of the bathroom, which gives Tom time to think about what to do with this unusual opportunity.

Tom remained in the stall, determined to see if Steve would come back. Sure enough, he came back in a couple of minutes. Now, as soon as Steve walked into the bathroom, Tom yelled out at him from the stall, "I said a couple of minutes, what in the heck is wrong with you? Are you some kind of weirdo or pervert?"

Steve looked extremely startled and started to say something, but Tom wouldn't give him the chance. He continued the tirade of yelling at him. Steve looked really freaked out, turned away from the stall, and started to leave the bathroom. When he opened the door to practically run out of the bathroom, Tom called out his name.

Steve turned back and said, "Excuse me?" Tom started laughing from inside the stall and then opened the door. Steve was absolutely dumbfounded. He could not believe what had just happened, and they both laughed for a minute or two. Steve agreed that the chances of him walking into that lounge, 'er bathroom, was one in a thousand. He went on in, and Tom went on his way. Just another fun moment in the life and times of the outside salesman. We always take advantage of spontaneous, humorous moments.

Large - Chicken - Breasts

One of the extra duties of the home improvement business is the processing of financial paperwork for those customers who do not pay cash. Sometimes we must go back to the customer's home after the sale for what we would call a remeasure. This is when we need to measure the windows, for example, closer than what the salesperson had measured. The old saying is to "measure twice and cut once." On one occasion, Jordan had to go to a home to remeasure the windows, and this is his story.

Jordan goes to the door of a normal, middle-class home and knocks on the door but does not hear a reply, so he knocks a second time. This time he hears someone holler, "Come in!" He slowly opens the door and announces himself. He is quick to notice a person lying in a bed within arm's reach of the front door. Here was the owner, lying on her back in bed, eating a bucket of fried chicken and watching television. Jordan introduces himself and explains why he is there. She tells him to go do what he needs to do and continues to lie in bed eating the chicken.

Jordan finishes his remeasuring of the windows and bids farewell to her while she is still in bed chomping on the bucket of chicken. He never did see her get out of that bed, but that bucket of chicken seemed to be bottomless. The bone pile on her television tray was getting high!

A couple of days later Jordan had to come back to get some finance paperwork signed and went through the same process, knocking on the door and hearing her holler, "Come in." He again opens the door and goes into the home. The same lady is lying in the same bed watching television.

Now, this woman was a large, heavyset person with a large, somewhat exposed bosom. Jordan was not trying to look at her chest, but some things are hard not to notice. As he passively views her chest, he notices that there is a piece of chicken meat lying in her cleavage. There was, however, no bucket of chicken to be seen this time.

His only thought as to where the piece of chicken came from was the bucket of chicken she was eating a couple days earlier. Could this be? Could she actually have been eating chicken and had a piece unknowingly drop into her cleavage and stay there for two or more days? Did she not shower or change clothes? It did appear that she looked the same as she did before. Maybe she got up to go to the bathroom and the chicken stayed lodged between her breasts.

You can call this gross, funny, or just weird, but it is definitely something you have to wonder about. I presume if she eventually found it later, she ate it!

Get Your Dad!

The same sales rep, Jordan, who had the fun of seeing two-day old chicken lying in someone's breasts, also had the fun of trying to get some finance papers signed at the Smiths' home. The Smiths were an older couple who needed to sign some finance papers, so Jordan went to their home hoping to meet a nice couple, get the papers signed promptly, and get back to the office.

When Jordan arrived at the home, he was met at the door by an adult-aged son, who looked like he had not showered or changed his clothes in a week. Jordan introduced himself and asked if he could meet with Mr. and Mrs. Smith for a moment to get signatures on some paperwork for their remodeling project.

The son mentioned that his mother was not feeling well and was lying in her bedroom. Jordan asked if she could meet him just for a moment or if he could take the papers in and get her signature. The son went into her bedroom to see if she was feeling okay enough to visit with Jordan. She said it would be okay for him to come into her bedroom and she would sign the papers. He went into her bedroom and was asked to sit in a chair next to her bed.

After he introduced himself and took care of the cordial greetings, Jordan asked if Mr. Smith could possibly join them. The mom hollered to her son, "Go get your dad!" With Jordan sitting next to the bed, his back to the door, he could hear the footsteps of someone coming into the room towards the bed.

Mrs. Smith looked toward the person coming into the bedroom and said, "Thanks for getting him." Her politeness seemed a little strange, considering how crass she was when asking her son to go get him. Within a second, the son says, "No problem, Mom." As Jordan was sitting next to the bed, waiting for Mr. Smith to come over and stand next to him, something came through the air over his shoulder and landed on the bed.

Jordan was startled by this object, but he was absolutely stunned when he saw it was Mr. Smith landing on the bed, belly up, and actually looking at him. No, Mr. Smith didn't jump on the bed. He was tossed on the bed by his son. Mr. Smith had no arms and little stubs for legs! He was merely a torso, having lost his limbs to medical issues.

It took all Jordan could muster up to keep himself from letting out an expletive, but needless to say, he was startled. Mr. Smith actually spoke to him and seemed relatively happy. Jordan was able to get the needed signatures from Mrs. Smith because she had power of attorney for her husband. With the paperwork signed, another sale was completed. Just another day in the wonderful world of home improvement sales. Believe it or not.

Buy or Die, Old Man

A good salesperson is always taught to make several offers when trying to negotiate a sale. Many potential customers need to say no a few times before they feel good about saying yes to an offer. Now, sometimes this negotiation process gets to be a little high pressured if the salesperson is relentless and the potential customer cannot say, "No, get out of my home!"

One high-pressured presentation occurred at a nice elderly couple's dining room table. The potential customers were a retired couple and, unfortunately, the husband, Jim, had need of an oxygen tank due to lung disease. Landon, the sales person, was sitting next to the husband. He had written an offer on the proposal form and then rolled his chair forward toward the husband while asking, "Shall we go ahead with that offer?" The husband looked at the offer, appeared to be thinking seriously about it, but then he started coughing and gasping, as if he couldn't breathe.

Landon rolled his chair back and asked Jim if he was all right. He replied, "Yes. I was just having trouble getting my breath." Landon and Jim's wife were both relieved, and so Landon moved back toward Jim and asked again, while pointing to the offer, "Well, can we move forward with this project?" Immediately Jim started coughing again.

He also started actually gasping for air and his face started turning a funny color. Landon again moved back away from Jim, and his wife again came to his aid, asking if they needed to call the doctor or take him to the hospital. Fortunately, though, Jim again regained his composure and started breathing normally. Landon was beginning to think these negotiations were too much for Jim.

Giving it one more college try, Landon moved his chair near Jim and asked one more time for the couple's business. Jim again started coughing and turning blue. His wife got out of her chair and immediately began fiddling with his air supply tube. She was frantically working with the equipment and asked Landon to call 911. Landon attempted to push his chair back away from the table so he could go to the phone and noticed it didn't easily move for him. He looked down to the floor to see if he was stuck on something, and sure enough, he was the cause of Jim's problem.

Landon had rolled his chair on top of Jim's oxygen line, cutting off the air supply. The line had become somewhat tangled on the bottom of Landon's chair. Landon hollered out that he sees the problem. They quickly untangled the line, and Jim was once again able to breathe normally. Talk about high pressure. Landon was rolling his chair over the top of Jim's air supply line after every offer, cutting his air off. He would give Jim air, present the offer, then cut the air off when asking for the business. I guess Landon could have been asking for Jim's business like this: "What do you say, Jim? Say yes to my offer and I will let you breathe. Say no and you will die." Now, that is high pressure sales.

Road Rage Rampage

Dave was a very seasoned home improvement representative who had worked as a manager for many years. With some changes in his company's organizational structure, he decided to go back to selling and leave the management chaos to others. Selling only versus selling and managing was going to hopefully relieve some stress in his daily life. All he had to do now was drive and talk for a living.

Dave was the master of the "take away—that's too much for you" selling technique. He would be showing someone his options for a new deck, and if he asked about a composite deck versus a wood deck, he would say, "You probably do not want to consider that option. It is too expensive for most people." Of course, the homeowner's ego would come out and would insist on seeing the better material.

Dave would grudgingly show the homeowner the more expensive option, price it out, and then close the sale by saying, "See, this price is too much for you, isn't it?" Of course, they couldn't say no, so Dave would write up the order and smile afterwards. This selling-only job seemed simple and easy to Dave, up until that one special day.

On a nice Tennessee afternoon, Dave was driving to an appointment a few miles outside of Knoxville. He had to take Interstate-40 for a few miles west of town, then exit, make a couple of turns, and he would then arrive at his assigned destination. The hard part was going to be the freeway traffic during the late afternoon. We all know how hectic the road can be when people are getting off work. Some think they have the right to any lane at any time and are in a hurry to get home. The south is NASCAR country, you know.

He had just pulled onto the freeway when another driver changed lanes in front of him, not allowing for a safe distance between them. Dave had to hit his brakes and abruptly slow down. Of course, aside from having to hit the brakes quickly, Dave also had to hit his horn as soon as this unsafe driver cut in front of him.

Well, this rude lane-changing driver thought Dave's horn honking was unnecessary, so he hit his brakes quickly too, just enough to make Dave have to brake to avoid hitting him. The road rage game was now officially on. Back and forth they went, cutting each other off, flipping each other the finger, and ticking each other off to no end. After a couple of miles, Dave, who was ahead of the crazy nut, had to exit the freeway. He thought he would be free of the maniac, but no such luck. The maniac exited the freeway a couple of cars behind him and was going the same way, seemingly following Dave.

Dave was thinking this was maybe a weird coincidence, but maybe the maniac was thinking about doing more than just honking at him. This was in the gun-toting state of Tennessee, so we have to be thinking this crazy guy could have a gun. They both continued making the same turns, going the same direction. After a couple of turns, Dave thought he should maybe go some other way on purpose, just to avoid a possible confrontation, but he was barely going to be on time for his appointment, so he stayed on course. Surely, he thought, this guy would go some other way soon.

Dave was apparently not going to be so lucky. They continued driving the same direction and making the same turns, right up to the same driveway. Dave pulled into his customer's driveway and the nutcase pulled in directly behind him. This was not going to be good.

They both got out of their cars, Dave a little slower than the other guy, thinking this idiot was going to shoot him. Dave quickly stated he was going to this address for an appointment and didn't want any trouble. The maniac driver looked Dave straight in the face and with a slow, angry tone states that this is his home. Dave was flabbergasted and blurted out, "Well, I guess this isn't going to work out." The homeowner and crazy driver exclaimed, "No, it isn't!" So, with no hesitation, Dave jumped back into his car and quickly left, having to drive around the homeowner's car. Sometimes we are conducting that all important warm-up without knowing it.

You Can't Imagine

In a small town east of Stockton, California is one of those homes that scares you as you walk up to it. The story starts with the dilapidated home being located on an unmapped dirt road, with no house number sign by the entrance and the driveway requiring a four-wheel drive vehicle to get over it safely. The house is virtually hidden by fifteen or so cars, trucks, boats, and whatnot. Animals are all around: cats, dogs, and some three-legged things. You have to ask yourself, "What the heck is this?"

The sales rep is Tom. The mission is to sell siding. Prejudging the appointment, not only was the home a scary place to be, but the chance of the homeowners having enough money for a twelve thousand dollar or more purchase looked slim. Tom, being a good salesman, continues on the narrow path to what he thinks is the front door, or he hopes. With a friendly knock and a long minute or so wait, a reasonable looking lady with plain, straight blond hair opens the door. She is expecting Tom and welcomes him into her home.

As mentioned earlier, the normal first step of most sales presentations is the warm-up, and Tom begins the process of trying to connect personally with the homeowner. He shares about his family tree story, hoping she might relate to it more than most. During the twenty-minute visit, Tom learns the lady owns a rental property. He is now thinking it might be an okay appointment. Maybe, just maybe, she does have some money to invest in her home. Tom gets her to start talking about her rental, and she starts to share the hassles she has with her tenants.

One previous tenant owed her money, and when she went to collect the past due rent, the defiant occupant would not open the door, and instead opened an upstairs window and hollered down at her. After some unpleasant words were shouted at each other, the tenant yelled, "Stay there, I'll be right down!" With the verbal banter now over and the tenant coming down, the owner turned her attention away from the upstairs window and looked at the front door.

The lesson here is to never believe a tenant who owes you money, because while the owner was waiting for the tenant to come down, a small—but big enough to hurt—window air conditioner was tossed out the upstairs window and hit the owner. Fortunately for the owner, it only glanced off her head, but it hit her shoulder, knocking her to the ground. Needless to say, the police came, chaos ensued, and a tenant went to jail for assault.

With this kind of story starting off the presentation, Tom knew he was in for an entertaining visit, to say the least. While he continues his warm-up, he learns she also has many, many cats. She informs him that she sometimes loses track of exactly how many cats she has and fears the coyotes had been getting a couple of them in the evening. She told one interesting cat story that was centered around her doing her laundry.

She had started drying a load of clothes and noticed that the dryer had stopped. Because she was watching television, she waited until a commercial started to go restart the load. When she went to the laundry area, she noticed the door had popped open, probably causing the dryer to stop. No big deal, she thought. After restarting the dryer, she went back to her television show.

After a couple of minutes, she heard a thumping noise in the dryer but thought it was merely an uneven load of wet laundry. This was probably why the door had opened before, shutting off the dryer. Well, guess what? The thumping noise was a cat that had jumped into the dryer when the door was open. She knew the cause of the noise was not going to be good because of the smell. The sad thing was she didn't really seem upset about losing a cat. It was just one of those unfortunate things that happen all too often in the country.

Tom was thinking, *This is one tough woman: living in the country by herself, being hit by an air conditioner, and burning a cat up in a dryer.* Not your normal, everyday occurrences, right? After another hour or so at the home, Tom is sitting at the kitchen table ready to start negotiating when suddenly, he notices a chicken in the kitchen. From out of nowhere, a chicken starts clucking away at Tom and the owner. This is simply one crazy appointment! The next thing Tom knows, there are two, then three chickens in the kitchen. He starts to focus on them and then realizes how they are getting in the house. They are coming through the wall!

Yep, this owner had a chicken door, 'er pet door, in her kitchen wall. Every day at about five in the evening, the chickens came through their pet door and into her kitchen for a feeding. Tom learns this happens twice a day, whether the owner is home or not. If she is gone, she merely sets some food and water out for them. Unfortunately, Tom did not sell the appointment, but he will remember this visit forever.

Driveway Bowling

East of Sacramento, California is a series of small towns, including Folsom, El Dorado Hills, and Cameron Park. For the most part, these towns are upscale suburbs with very nice homes. However, there is always the exception to any rule, and this area was not exempt from the norms of society. In between these towns are a few hills, some dirt roads, and of course, a couple of mobile luxury homes. What is a mobile luxury home, you ask? Well, that is when you take three single-wide mobile homes, put them side-by-side long ways, remove the walls in between them, and put a common roof over the top!

Sure as shootin', Tom drives through this nice upscale neighborhood, then turns to go up this somewhat paved road. Just past the old 1970's station wagon, hidden behind some never-mowed weeds, he finds a mailbox with the house number of his siding appointment. Yes, it was a mobile luxury home. Tom stood outside for a moment, just to soak it all in—to enjoy the irony of the neighborhood. Then he proceeds to go do the finest presentation he could. On the way up to the home, he notices several oddities, one of which was a bowling ball laying near the driveway. When was the last time you saw a bowling ball next to a driveway?!

He knocks on the door and is cordially invited into the "luxury" home. The couple was very nice, and they had a couple of teenage children in the living room watching television. Vinyl siding is on the homeowners' minds, so Tom goes through the presentation and ends up selling a siding project. After completing the paperwork, a typical sales person always does what we call a warm-down. This is when we change the subject to something other than the project and let everyone come back to reality. As part of the warm-down, Tom asks in a polite, friendly manner, whose bowling ball was out in the driveway.

Immediately, the husband mentions it is his and starts cussing the kids out! He was not happy to hear that his lucky bowling ball was outside again. The wife chimes in that the kids seem to enjoy playing a particular game with it outside. The funny thing was he still used the ball, nicks and all. Apparently, he belongs to a bowling league and it was his pride and joy ball.

The wife began to share the game the kids primarily like to play with his bowling ball. You could see the husband fuming over each line of her narrative. He was steaming mad! Tom sat in wonder as the story unfolded. Apparently, the kids liked to take the ball and roll it down the driveway to the intersection below and knock some "pins" down. Their idea of pins was anything they could find in the yard, like boxes, toys, and so on. The hard part of the game was trying to stop the ball at the bottom of the hill before it flew into the neighbor's house.

I imagine that a twelve- to fifteen pound bowling ball going down a relatively steep driveway for forty feet or so probably gains some speed. Well, one time the kids rolled it down the driveway and a neighborhood kid, who apparently wasn't familiar with this game, saw the ball coming down the driveway and decided it would be fun to go kick the ball back up the driveway.

You can imagine this train wreck. The kid runs full speed at the ball and kicks it toe-first before anyone could warn him. Not that I would have when I was that age. So just like an animated cartoon, the kid kicks the bowling ball and immediately screams in pain, as he had flipped over the front of the ball directly onto his face. He is screaming while holding his broken toe. After holding his toe for a second, his hands go to his face to check on the bleeding that was caused when he face-planted on the ground. The other kids were all laughing their heads off. What a scene! Of course, the bowling ball kept going downhill, but nobody bothered to chase it. They were all falling on their backs laughing at the idiot who just kicked a bowling ball. The wounded kid's mother was not very pleased about her son's demise, and she apparently lit into the mother of the bowling team.

Meanwhile, the husband who was agonizing over the demise of his prize bowling ball broke a smile and shook his head in disbelief. Just another day in the life of the home improvement salesperson.

Twister Anyone?

In California, there is a town by the name of Davis, and the people there tend to be a little unique. In some circles, the town is referred to as "The People's Republic of Davis." The main point is you that shouldn't be too surprised who you meet when working there. Tom went on an appointment there with a lady who was elderly and rather snobby. As soon as he went into her home, he noticed a rather pungent smell. It was tolerable but not very pleasant. She tried to act like she had a lot of money and always wanted the best quality of products for her home, but she could not afford a maid or Lysol.

After she told Tom how wonderful her life had been and how she has always had the good things in life, Tom went outside to measure the average-looking home for new siding. When he went out through the sliding-glass door off the dining room, he noticed a pile of something. This pile was about a foot high and a foot in diameter. Tom thought nothing about it, assuming it was dirt or something that she dumped out, like cigarette ashes. When Tom went back inside, he started to put two and two together. He noticed she had a couple of cats, and then he noticed she had stains on her carpet. When one of the cats stopped at one of the stains, smelled it, then proceeded to dump a load, Tom knew the rest of the story.

There is an old saying, "One man's pet-stained carpet is another man's Twister game." Apparently, this old lady liked to play Twister because Tom realized that this unique lady was scooping the poop off her carpet and dumping it outside of her sliding door. That pile of stuff was really a pile of cat poop. People who let their cats poop on the carpet, then just scrape it off and put it on the back steps should not be allowed to buy siding. No sale was made that day. She was a nice lady, but she could not afford to buy siding for her house, nor could she afford a cat box.

I guess it was a good thing Tom did not step in that pile; otherwise, he would have been playing Twister with an eighty year-old woman.

WHERE'S THE FRONT DOOR?

Briggs was driving to an appointment in Redding, California, and at the end of a road were three trailer homes. None of the homes had house numbers, so it was difficult to know which house to visit. One house looked like an actual junkyard. There was so much junk around the house, you could not tell where the front door was located. After knocking on a couple of doors in the neighborhood, Briggs learned that his potential customer was the person who owned the junkyard trailer.

Briggs did not believe anybody lived in the trailer, but a neighbor confirmed it was where the man lived. Since there was so much garbage in front of the trailer, some of it coming halfway up to the front door, he thought the owner entered through the sliding back door. Briggs looked around the back of the trailer and could not see any steps to the sliding back door. Scratching his head, he went to the front of the trailer and stood there looking at it for several minutes. Finally, he noticed on top of the garbage was a beaten-down path to a sliding window. Could that be caused by someone walking on top of the pile?

Out of curiosity, Briggs decided to park his truck up the road and wait to see if the homeowner would come home. After about thirty minutes, a person drove down the road, parked by the trailer, and then climbed over the garbage and went into the trailer through the window. Now, we could say that Briggs was a weak salesperson, but he decided not to climb over the garbage and knock on a window to go inside. Could you imagine what the inside looked like?

Depends Are Dependable

In the world of sales, closing ratios and returns per appointment are statistics that must be tracked. Sales reps must be held accountable for their results. One time, a sales rep by the name of Brian tried to get his previous day's appointment removed from his results. His manager asked him for a reason, and here is what Brian said had happened.

Brian started to explain about this nice older gentleman whose wife had passed away a couple of years before. This gentleman seemed to be of fragile health but wanted to still take care of his home. He was interested in vinyl siding and listened intently to Brian's presentation. Partway through Brian's presentation, Brian started to smell a noxious odor. He thought the man had merely passed gas. Once the homeowner noticed the smell too, he said to Brian, "Please excuse me. I must change my Depends." This nice old man had just pooped himself.

Brian told the gentleman that he would just see himself out, and maybe he could call Brian's company if he was still interested. Brian did not have the heart to stay there and continue the presentation. When Brian reported that he did not give a full presentation because the man had pooped himself, the management staff said that was not a good enough excuse. They charged him for the lead and wanted him to go back the next day and finish the presentation. Would you have the moxy to go back?

Our Alternative Lifestyle Friends

In the next few stories, we are going to share some of the fun our alternative lifestyle citizens have had with our sales team. This is not intended to be disparaging or disrespectful. We simply found a lot of fun situations and stories that were quite entertaining.

A sales rep named George lived in a progressive town in Colorado. On one appointment, he met with a single gentleman who was middle-aged and quite friendly. George was in the middle of his siding presentation and needed to go outside to get some measurements. After about twenty minutes outside, he went back into the house and found the homeowner sitting naked at the table with two glasses of wine next to him.

I don't know about you, but I'm not sure if there is any sales training that covers this situation. Could you imagine a sales training class with two people role playing that scenario? George was flabbergasted and tried to be polite but excused himself from the home. We never ask people to put themselves into dangerous or uncomfortable situations. George politely said he was short on time and had to leave. He was of course charged with the appointment and was given a hard time about not selling siding to the homeowner. The attitude of the company is that every appointment can be sold by someone. Would you have stayed?

Terry Needs to Decide

There was a siding salesperson by the name of Terry, who was not married and for some reason seemed to attract members of the gay community on a regular basis. Regardless of your sexual orientation, you hopefully can see how this would be humorous. Actually, the previous story was shared with me by my gay assistant manager, who found it hilarious.

On one occasion, Terry ran an appointment in northern California with both homeowners being male. This couple was openly gay, but Terry was not bothered by sexual choice, so he went through his normal process. As he started his presentation, he noticed that one of the men seemed to be rather friendly with him. In fact, this man was hitting on Terry, making such sexual comments as, "You have a nice butt."

When Terry went outside to measure the home for installing siding, this man followed him out. The sexual advances continued despite the man's partner being present. They got to the point where Terry was back inside discussing the finer details of the project when this man said to Terry, "I could take you on this table, right now."

Terry finally had enough, saying he had run out of time and had to leave the home. For some reason, this man followed Terry outside the house, slapped him on the buttocks, and told him he was welcome back any time. Terry did not go back but did make the mistake of sharing the story with his peers and assistant manager at work. This may have just been a one-time chuckle among the staff, but he had another unusual experience that was along the same lines.

One time, Terry was sick from a cold, and when he came back to work, he had to ride with our trainer on a couple of appointments before he could go on his own appointments. This policy was to help the person who had missed work get back into the selling mode before they run their own appointments. Most appointments cost the company about two hundred to four hundred dollars apiece, whether they sell or not. So, Terry went on an appointment with our trainer, Jeff, to get back into the swing of things before going on his own appointments. When they got to the house, the homeowner met Jeff outside. He would not let Jeff into the house for some reason and made him present outside in the driveway.

The rep and the homeowner pulled some chairs out from the garage and put them in front of the garage door. Terry was still coughing and sniffling at times, so he stayed down the driveway near the sidewalk. He did not want to start coughing and interrupt Jeff's presentation. While Terry was standing at the bottom of the driveway, still within hearing distance of the sales presentation, a man came down the sidewalk and stopped beside Terry. He looked at Terry, smiled, and then asked him if he had a tissue. Terry thought he had seen the tissue that he was coughing into, so he said, "No I don't. I only have this one." Terry turned away from the man to continue listening to Jeff's presentation to the homeowner. The man who had approached Terry did not leave. He stayed right next to him. Can you say, "creeper?"

The man once again asked if Terry had a tissue and stepped closer to Terry, looking at him intensely. Terry once again told him he did not have one to spare. He then started to think the man was asking for some type of drug. Since the man did not leave, Terry made the mistake of looking at him and smiled. The man must have thought this was an invitation because he stepped closer to him, reached out, touched Terry's tie, and said, "That is a nice tie." He pulled the tie toward himself and kissed it with passion. Yep, the stranger kissed his tie. Now, Terry was getting mad and wanted to say something to the man, but he did not because Jeff was still presenting.

The stranger again asked Terry if he had a tissue. At the point of going postal, Terry stated in a stern manner, "No!" Out of frustration, Terry finally said to the man, "Here's a tissue, go away!" He handed the man his used tissue. The man quickly took the tissue, put it down the front of his pants and starting rubbing himself. The man seemed to be enjoying himself. Terry freaked out, told the man he had to leave, and slightly pushed him. The man pulled out the tissue and offered it back to him. Terry told him emphatically, "No!" Thankfully, the man did leave, but Terry was messed up for life. To this day, you never want to tell him he has a nice tie.

Terry, of course, made the same mistake of sharing this story with his peers and trainer. After having two episodes of this nature in a short time, people were asking Terry if he preferred an alternative lifestyle. It wasn't but a couple of months later that Terry announced he was engaged to a woman. Not that there is anything wrong with that.

ANDREW MAKES A NEW BEST FRIEND

After working several years in California, I acquired many alternative-lifestyle friends and associates. Having grown up in the 70's, I learned to like people based on their personal honesty and behaviors, not their personal lifestyle. For the most part, I have always had a positive experience with most people who live an alternative lifestyle from what many consider the mainstream.

One of the roofing appointments I went on in Sacramento was for a gentleman named Steve. He lived in what was considered a historical home in east Sacramento, and special care had to be taken to preserve many of the exterior features of his home. I personally love old homes and antiques, so we got along immediately because we had a common interest in his home.

Steve gave me a tour of his historical home, showed me pictures of his partner, and when he saw that I was not nervous or prejudice, we became very open in our conversation. Now Steve, was an openly gay person who showed no embarrassment regarding his lifestyle. Feeling a sense of trust between us, I asked Steve if he would like to help me pull a great joke on our best roofing installer, Anthony.

Now Anthony, was a serious homophobe who was very uncomfortable being around anyone who was gay. I asked Steve if he would help me prank him by being very "friendly" when he came out to work on Steve's home. Steve knew exactly what to do and was very excited about the opportunity to play with Anthony's phobia.

To get this prank started, I went back to our company's office and told the owner, who was a best friend of mine, what I had set up. He thought this would be hilarious and gladly chipped in on the prank. The roofing installation was scheduled, and we sent Anthony over to get started on the project, with great anticipation for what was to come. Steve did not let us down! The owner of the roofing company, Chris, and I were anxiously waiting in our company's office that late afternoon on the day Anthony started working on Steve's roof. We heard Anthony pull up to the front of our office, stop abruptly, exit his truck and slam the door. He came quickly in to meet us, carrying with him a look of pure frustration. In a matter of seconds, he began to tell us what went on that day.

"You would not believe what happened to me today!" he exclaimed. We acted totally dumbfounded and asked him to explain. Anthony continued, "You know that roof job you sent me on? That Steve guy? Well, he is gay!" Andy was so exasperated, that he practically hyperventilated. What a hoot! We, of course, acted like we knew nothing and were sincerely interested in the details—which, of course, we were! Anthony went on to explain how Steve had invited him into his house, showed him pictures of his partner, then took Anthony into his bedroom to show him a possible leak from the roof. It took all of the energy he had not to freak out directly in front of Steve.

This project went on for about one week, and every day we heard more complaints about Steve and his gayness (as Anthony described it). We kept laughing at Anthony and never told him that I had set the week of torture up for him. After the job was completed, I went by Steve's house to thank him for his business and to give him the report on Anthony's anxiety breakdown. Steve and I both laughed and celebrated with a couple of sodas.

After the job was completed, we went ahead and told Anthony what we had done to him. He called us a couple of extreme vulgarities and stormed out of the office. He eventually calmed down, but this remained a sore spot between us for quite a while.

A funny follow-up to this story occurred about a year or so later, when Anthony got married. Like many newly married couples, he and his wife had a nice wedding photo of the two of them framed and placed on an easel for the family and wedding guests to sign.

I could not resist the temptation to continue our joke, so in one little space on the wedding photo, I wrote the name "Steve" with xoxoxo afterwards. I told only the roofing company owner about this new prank. It was probably a full two months later when Anthony again pulled up quickly in front of our office and stormed inside to confront us. He started with, "You lousy @#!#!! You ruined my wedding photo!"

"What do you mean?" I replied.

"You #$@#$@ signed our photo with Steve's name and put xoxoxo afterwards!"

"Are you sure he didn't attend?" I asked while laughing. This ticked Anthony off even more, and he kept going back to how I ruined his photo. He said he told his wife about Steve and how horrible that week was, working on his roof. Our reply to Anthony was, "Why did you tell your wife who he was?"

I think if we were to bring this up to Anthony today, he would probably get horribly upset and possibly punch me or whoever mentioned it. I think we will let Anthony have his peace and let this one fade into the sunset, for now.

The Jokes We Play

Playing jokes on fellow home improvement associates was a fairly routine practice. We were always looking for a laugh or two to break up the forty thousand miles a year we drove and the late nights we worked. One joke Tom pulled was on Jeff, who was a young man in his early twenties and new to the home improvement industry. This was unfortunate for him but quite fortunate for us sales veterans. The company's owner always wanted the older, more experienced salespeople to help the new rookies, so at times we would take one of them along on a presentation for them to watch and learn.

Of course, the fun part was between appointments, when we would go to lunch or dinner. Sometimes if two or three reps were in the same town, we would all try to meet together for lunch or dinner. One time we were meeting in Modesto, California, and we went to a restaurant to eat with about six people. One of these six reps was Jeff, a young, good-looking guy who considered himself a ladies man. He was going to be an easy mark for this joke. As we went to place our orders, Tom went first and mentioned to the attendant who took our order to be careful of the tall guy at the end of the line.

The young, teenage lady behind the counter asked us why she needed to be careful of him. Tom told her he had been in trouble once for asking young teenage girls out on dates and was actually arrested; he has also been charged once for possession of child pornography and was on Meghan's list. We told her that because she was cute, he might try to be friendly with her and possibly ask her out. We strongly advised her to be short with him and not get into any lengthy conversation with him.

As all of us placed our orders, we went and sat at the table, leaving young Jeff at the counter alone with the young teenage girl. As we watched Jeff trying to be friendly with her, you could tell she was nervous and trying not to make eye contact with him. Jeff kept talking and being persistent. However, she gave him the cold shoulder, and he left knowing something was wrong.

When Jeff came over to the table to sit with us, he saw we were laughing and he abruptly dropped his tray on the table and said to us, "All right, what am I, who am I, and what did you say to her?" As we laughed out loud, we told Jeff he was a pedophile and that she should try to avoid him. We of course started laughing, but Jeff didn't think it was too funny. From that point on, whenever we saw a young girl, we said to Jeff, "Hey, Jeff, don't try to pick her up, she is too young for you." Some people may think this joke was mean, but in our social group, we thought it was funny.

It Is Only a Memory Jogger

Training new sales reps in a classroom setting is often quite challenging. I worked as a national sales trainer for a company that flew their new reps in from out of state to attend a formal one-week training class. The reps were told it was a serious course with daily testing, and if they did not do well, they could fail the course and be dismissed from the company. You would think this warning would cause a new employee to focus and take the training seriously. However, if you lived in Minnesota and it was wintertime, you might think, if I get hired, I will get a week's vacation in sunny California. Some did come to class to study hard and learn, but some were just too stupid to learn anything, no matter how hard they tried. One of the latter students was taking a test one day, and the senior trainer, whose name was Jody, sat at the front of the room watching the students. During most testing, I would sit in my office in the back of the training room with the door open so that I could see the class.

One time, I noticed that Michael would look toward Jody, to see if he was looking in his direction. If he wasn't, Michael would take his thumb, pull out his shirt pocket, and look into it. I thought this was a little strange, so I went up to Jody and shared my observation regarding Michael. Jody waited for a minute, then got up from his chair, and casually walked around the room.

He worked his way toward Michael's table and stood behind him. With Jody standing one foot behind him, Michael once again read a test question and then looked in his shirt pocket. Jody noticed a piece of paper in the shirt pocket and asked Michael, "What is in your shirt pocket?" Michael, with no hesitation and totally calm, said to Jody, "Oh that is nothing; it is just a memory jogger."

Apparently, a memory jogger is not a cheat sheet. Jody, while laughing, said a memory jogger was cheating and asked Michael to give him the paper. Needless to say, Michael didn't last very long in the home improvement industry. He never could learn how to sell, but at least he knew how to cheat. If we hadn't fired him, he probably would have been one of those sales reps who lied and made up crap just to make a sale. Jody and I still laugh about Michael and his memory jogger.

BAM! DID YOU SEE THAT?

Jody, the sales trainer I mentioned before, was a veteran of the home improvement industry. He had literally sold millions of dollars of home improvements, and I considered it a privilege to work with him as a sales trainer. He had great insight, referenced several published sales trainers——many who he personally knew— and he always had great analogies to help make a point. One of the lessons Jody taught us was to never cut out any part of your presentation because you never knew what part of your presentation was going to influence the potential customer to buy. To help us remember this important sales tip, Jody shared the following story.

Because of Jody's success with residential sales, he was offered a managerial position in Texas. Some people thought he was nuts to move from California to Texas during the banking-crisis downfall, and they didn't mind telling him such. They told him the economy was bad, and he would fail as a manager. Jody just ignored them and kept thinking about an old saying a famous trainer taught him: "Attitude is everything!"

Jody took his positive attitude to Texas and first surveyed the sales team he inherited. He met with them one-on-one and asked them if they believed they could be successful. Ninety percent of the existing reps said they thought the economy was too bad for them to really be successful, so he fired all but one. He then hired reps who believed they could make sales. Jody believed he could teach them to sell if their attitude was right. So with a new team and a great attitude, Jody went to work.

One of his appointments early on was with a retired couple supposedly interested in buying new siding for their home. As the presentation was moving along, Jody tried to get the wife involved by asking her questions, but she didn't want anything to do with vinyl siding. She thought her husband was stupid for setting up the appointment in the first place. Every time Jody asked her to help hold something or participate in some way, she would shrug her shoulders, grunt a little, and say that she wasn't interested or didn't care.

The husband though, was very interested in getting vinyl siding because he didn't want to have to paint the house again. With every new feature he learned about, the husband became more anxious to buy. Jody knew he had the husband sold, but he hadn't won over the wife yet. He had been taught to always try to get both the husband and wife involved in the presentation, so he persisted in asking the wife what she thought of this feature or that benefit. Nothing seemed to get her attention until they came to the part in the presentation where Jody would show that the new vinyl siding he was selling would not easily stain.

To show this feature of the product, Jody would take the old red iodine your mother used to put on your sores or cuts and put a little bit of it on some vinyl siding. His part of the demonstration started by using a poor quality of vinyl siding first. Jody would put some of the red iodine onto the cheaper product and ask the homeowners if they would wipe it off with a paper towel. After Jody put the iodine on the siding, he asked the wife to try and wipe it off. She would grudgingly try to wipe it off and murmur, "It doesn't come off." The wife reacted the same way when Jody then demonstrated on a couple of the older, poorer quality sidings. It then came time to put the iodine on the new siding Jody was trying to sell. It was a much better quality of product, so the results were going to be different.

Staying true to the sales technique of involving both the husband and wife, Jody again asked the wife to wipe the iodine off the new siding. When she tried to wipe the iodine off the new siding, she noticed it did come off and left no stain. Right after she wiped off the iodine, her eyes got big and she looked at the siding and then elbowed her husband, who was sitting on a stool next to her. She knocked her husband completely off the stool onto the floor and said to him while pointing her finger at him, "You see that, those little SOBs' will not be able to melt their crayons on our house anymore!"

Apparently, the neighborhood brats were taking crayons and melting them on the hot aluminum siding. Needless to say, the couple bought the siding, and Jody continued to laugh for many years after that presentation. Any time some new trainee would tell Jody he didn't see why they needed to do that step of the presentation, Jody would say, "Well, let me share a quick story with you about a couple in Texas." As a side note, Jody's office became extremely successful, and he was promoted once again.

The Rodeo Charity Event

One late afternoon, three sales reps, Dan, Patrick, and Tom, went to a restaurant to have dinner. They invited the new rep Jeff, along to have dinner with them. The entrance to the restaurant had a hostess podium and an adjacent room with a pool table. Because there was a thirty to forty-five minute wait to get a table, the four reps decided to shoot some pool. Jeff was a little shy, being new, so they had to coax him into shooting pool with them. The combination of Dan, Patrick and Tom was a very dangerous one. These three sales people were older, well paid, and not shy. While they were playing pool, four women came into the restaurant and put their names on the waiting list for a table.

For some reason, these four women started singing a song together while the sales reps were trying to shoot pool. After they finished singing the song, the men at the pool table gave them a little applause and said, "That was really good." Now, I don't remember which one of the salespeople made the offer, but he asked the women to sing a song specifically for them while they shot pool. Jeff was sitting there amazed at the boldness of these veteran sales reps. He stayed quiet and just sat in his chair smiling.

The four women came over by the pool table, and while the men were playing pool, they sang a song by the Beach Boys. They were exceptionally good at singing together, so Tom went over to them after they finished their song and gave them a ten-dollar bill, saying, "Thanks for singing to us. You girls are quite talented." The women looked at each other and then asked if they could sing some more to us. The reps gladly let them sing for them, and the women ended up making about sixty dollars while they waited to get into the main dining area.

Jeff was stunned that they would pay the women to sing to them while they played pool. The veterans thought it was interesting and fun to have four women singing to them while playing. Apparently, these four women were a quartet who sang together. They were in Sacramento for a choral festival the following day.

The reps were having so much fun playing pool, they asked for their dinner to be brought out to the pool table area. The managers thought that would be okay since it was so crowded that night. So, with the singing quartet gone, the men had to find something new to entertain themselves. Now, Patrick was single and somewhat of a ladies' man. That night, he was wearing a cowboy shirt that looked rather fancy, and he had a nice pair of cowboy boots on as usual.

Dan and Tom came up with an idea that when women came into the restaurant, they would offer them the opportunity for a dollar to sign Patrick's shirt and give him a kiss. The sales pitch they gave the women who came into the restaurant was that since Patrick was well known in the rodeo world, he was going to collect signatures on his shirt as a way to raise money for the rodeo. Of course, this was not true, but they wanted to see if they could pull it off.

As women came into the restaurant, Dan and Tom took turns selling Patrick's shirt for signing and pimping him out for a kiss. They collected over twenty dollars, and each of them who paid, signed Patrick's shirt. When the sales reps left the restaurant, they divided up the money between the three, and they all had a good laugh. Jeff, the rookie, was astonished and could not believe what he just witnessed. He, of course, did not get any money since he hadn't contributed to the cause.

Jeff asked Dan if this was a common type of evening entertainment. Dan said it was and told him he had done worse. For example, one time, Dan posed as a Hanes pantyhose representative to engage women in conversations about their pantyhose. Dan told Jeff that sometimes the girls would lift up their dresses and show their legs to him. If you ever find yourself going out to dinner with home improvement salespeople, be very careful and prepared for the unknown.

Man Talking to His Dead Wife

In Auburn, California, Stratton was running an appointment and the appointment details indicated that he was visiting a couple. This particular visit was for the possible installation of new siding on the couple's home. When Stratton arrived at the appointment, the husband answered the door and invited him into his home. After a few minutes of conversation, Stratton asked if his wife would be joining them. The husband said she was not available, so Stratton proceeded with his presentation.

After an hour or so, it came time to discuss the possible new color of the siding for their home. The husband picked out a color, saying he thought his wife would like that particular one. Stratton asked if we would have the chance to show it to her, and the husband said, "Sure, let me ask her; she is right there." Stratton turned to look for the wife and did not see anyone. The husband looked in the direction of the hallway and asked her if she would like the color. Apparently, she said the color he picked would be fine with her.

Stratton looked twice and thrice, but there was nobody there and he heard no answer. It then dawned on him: The husband was either delusional or he was talking to a ghost. Unfortunately, Stratton learned that the man's wife had passed away recently and he was having some issues. Once Stratton realized this, he quickly and politely left the home and did not push for a sale. Sometimes, you have to say no for the potential customer if that potential customer may not be able to make a rational decision.

To the Rescue

Sometimes a sales appointment can take a rep to the countryside, away from the city. The drive is often beautiful and quite relaxing. This part of the business is sometimes just what the doctor ordered. We often would visit a country setting of homes in the foothills of the Sierras or over near the Napa Valley. We would often end up in a subdivision with nice homes on large five-plus acre tracts. There may be ten to twenty homes in these subdivisions, quite large in size, with covered porches, white or yellow paint, a few horses, a dog or two, and well, you get the picture.

One winter day, Dan was on such an appointment attempting to sell vinyl siding to a nice retired couple. After a couple of hours, Dan had written a contract for the project and was going through the warm-down process. This is what salespeople do after the contracts are written, in an attempt to get the customers relaxed and thinking about something other than the ten thousand dollar-plus commitment they just made. As Dan was taking some of his materials out to his car, the homeowners came out onto the porch and continued with their conversation.

Things were going well, and everyone was happy and relaxed, so Dan felt his contract was secure with a low chance of cancellation.

While listening to his new customers, Dan thought he heard a small cry or voice coming from somewhere in the yard. Because the yard was so large, he could not pin the location down. Again, and again, Dan heard this voice, and to him it sounded like someone calling for help. He asked the homeowners to listen and see if they could hear it too. At first, they said they didn't hear it. Dan was positive he heard something, so they all started listening quite intently.

Soon everyone could agree they heard something like a person calling for help in a very distressed manner. As they all started walking around the yard trying to pin the voice down, they found themselves leaving the customer's property and going toward their neighbor's home. They continued across the neighbor's property, up to the house and around to the front porch area. Here, to their surprise and horror, they found that the single, elderly neighbor had fallen off the porch somehow, and was injured to the point where she could not get up by herself.

Dan called 911, and within a few minutes an ambulance came to help the injured woman. It was by pure luck or a guiding hand that Dan stayed on the front porch of his new customers and heard this faint voice calling for help. In Dan's attempt to save his sale, he helped save a person's life. With it being winter, this lady probably would have died that evening, lying out in the cold winter night.

NOT ME!

Spencer was a young, eighteen year-old sales rep for our company, and even though he was young, he looked like a person people could trust, and this made him rather effective as a sales person. One of the steps salespeople take when selling is to review the three-day right of rescission. Homeowners have a legal right to be informed of this when a salesperson comes to your home to sell you any service.

Some salespeople go over this form lightly, trying to make it seem like an unimportant step in the process. Others like to review the form in an upfront manner, being rather frank about the idea that the new customer could back out of the sale. For those like Spencer, who take this more upfront approach, the process went like this, but with a twist at the end.

When it came time to review the Right to Cancel form, Spencer mentioned to the couple that they had three days to consider their decision, and they could cancel it during this time. Spencer said to the married couple, "Folks, if either of you have any reservations about going forward with this project, I would really rather know right now." Spencer then went into silent mode and waited for a response. He was well trained!

The husband looked at Spencer, then looked back at his wife, and said he was okay with everything and mentioned that he was looking forward to changing their home's appearance. The wife looked at the contract, looked at Spencer, looked at her husband, looked at the contract, and then said, "Not me! You know what, I am not signing anything else. In fact, I do not want to do this, and I do not want to be married to you anymore. I am going to file for divorce!"

She got up from the table, grabbed her purse, and walked out of the house, leaving the husband and Spencer sitting there, staring at each other, and then staring at the door she just went out. Unfortunately, Spencer had just lost the sale and the husband just lost his wife. Not knowing what to do with the situation, Spencer quickly excused himself from the home and left. I guess we didn't train him well enough!

When Spencer came back to the office and reviewed the presentation with his manager, the manager suggested that Spencer still could have sold the project because if the husband kept the house, he would still need the siding, and if they had to sell their home, they could sell it quicker with the new siding on it and probably get more money for it. The motto of the company was that someone could have made the sale, regardless of the situation. If you want to test the strength of your marriage, just try buying a major home improvement.

KURT AND HIS WEIRD STORIES

Have you ever heard about people who always seem to be lucky? Or maybe someone who is always unlucky? Well, my friend Kurt was like a magnet when it came to having strange encounters of a third kind. He was usually good for one weird story a month. Why him? We never figured it out so, we just sat back and enjoyed the humor.

Often salespeople drive long distances to a home and wonder, "Why did this person ever set this appointment?" We run appointments and find out they do not have any money, just filed for bankruptcy, or they are unemployed, yet they set an appointment to buy something that will cost thousands of dollars. In most cases, these potential customers pull out the excuse card at the end of the sales presentation, saying the project is just too much money. Well, duh! They don't have a job! In reality, they couldn't buy a movie ticket without borrowing the money. Now, as we sometimes say in the South, "Bless their heart!" Maybe, these people are lonely or just optimistic, we don't know, but they are common in the home improvement business.

One time, Kurt went on a siding appointment on a dark winter night in the countryside of northern California. The home was a somewhat simple one-story home with old wood siding. It was in desperate need of remodeling, so the opportunity looked good for Kurt. The homeowner was a single man who actually seemed to be qualified to buy new siding for his home. He had a reasonably valued property, looked reasonable, and he had a job. Kurt was excited to have what seemed to be a real opportunity. He proceeded with his presentation, and everything was going well, when for no explained reason the man excused himself from the kitchen table and went into the back of his home.

Kurt thought he was either going to the bathroom or maybe needed to get something relevant to the presentation, like a photo or a color sample. However, after about five minutes, the man had not returned, and Kurt could not hear any sounds in the back. After about 10 minutes, Kurt stood up and called for the homeowner by name, to no reply.

After fifteen minutes or so, he began to think *this is getting really weird*, so he called the owner's name out again, and no response. Kurt was now getting worried, so he called another rep and good friend named Doc. He explained the situation, and Doc suggested Kurt pack up his things, then leave and call the cops. Concerned for the homeowner's well-being, Kurt agreed and did exactly that. Once he got into his car, he first called the homeowner and but got no answer.

Fearing the worst, Kurt called the police and explained what happened. The police agreed to call the homeowner and then report back to him what they learn. Kurt was afraid the owner may have had a heart attack or something, and he didn't want to be accused of doing anything wrong. About five to ten minutes passed, and the police finally called back and informed him that they reached the homeowner and everything seemed to be okay. The owner had simply had enough and didn't want to hear anymore, nor did he have the guts to ask Kurt to leave. He just walked away!

Now, this was the first time any of us salespeople had ever heard of a homeowner actually being unable to say no to a salesperson. This weak prospect just walked away and never came back. From then on, we started asking the question of homeowners, "You can just say no to our offer, correct?" We do run into all types in our profession.

On another visit, Kurt went to a home occupied by Catholic nuns. Kurt was always polite and pleasant, but he was also a closer. He did not want to leave the home without a sale, so he was always persistent. At the end of the visit, the nuns said they wanted to pray about their decision now that they had information to consider. After some conversation along the lines of, "Wouldn't God want you to take advantage of this great promotion and save thousands of dollars?" and "Could we pray about it now?" Kurt managed to upset the peaceful nuns, and they kicked him out of their home. Only Kurt could have this happen to him!

Another time, Kurt was driving down a two-lane highway near the Sierra Mountains, when all of a sudden something hit his driver's side window. Kurt quickly glanced at the window and saw the face of a mountain lion smashed into his window. He didn't stop to see if it was okay, but we never could figure out how or why it had happened. He also ended up with bullet holes in his car door, as he was almost a victim of random, misdirected gunfire. Only Kurt...

EMERGENCY FIRST-AID

In the wonderful state of Tennessee, you will find many down-to-earth—sometimes you think grown from the dirt—people who love the great outdoors. This is why you can buy any piece of clothing with a camouflage pattern, including underwear. Hunting and fishing is very common in this beautiful state and being called a redneck is considered a compliment.

One beautiful autumn day, Tom was visiting a couple who was not from Tennessee. They had decided to move there for the natural beauty and outdoor activities and stayed here because they loved the relaxed atmosphere (and no state income tax). The sales appointment was for enclosing a car porch and creating a sunroom so they could enjoy the wooded surroundings more often. It was such a nice day, they just sat outside and discussed the options for their project.

During the presentation, the wife left for another engagement and the husband stayed to get the estimate. After the presentation was about halfway completed, Tom and the owner were sitting in the car porch area when they noticed a large shadow in the air passing by, screeching loudly. Immediately, after turning their attention toward the loud noise, they heard a thumping sound near the house. Looking to the wooded side of the car porch, they noticed a big hawk flying up into the trees. Admiring the big bird, the two then noticed a small black bird lying on the ground next to a small bush near the house.

The bird was alive but obviously in shock or had the wind knocked out of him (we presumed it was a boy bird). The owner, who loves the outdoors and animals, was greatly concerned for the bird, so he picked it up and tried to calm it down. Apparently, the hawk was chasing the bird, and it flew directly into a house window. After holding the bird and speaking sweet nothings to it for a minute, the man began to blow into the bird's face, trying to help it breathe. The bird continued to have very strained breathing and was not improving, so the homeowner started the usual procedure of mouth-to-mouth resuscitation.

He actually put his mouth over the bird's beak and tried to blow air into "him." Tom really didn't see any improvement in the bird from this procedure, but the homeowner continued for about two minutes. At this point, Tom decided the two of them needed to be alone, so he excused himself and left the home. As they say in the South, "Bless his heart for trying to help that bird!" If you really understand the "bless his heart" phrase, it is not a compliment but a nice way of saying one is an idiot or stupid. He must have been a damn Yankee because the locals would have fed that bird to the hawk or fried it up for a snack.

Gotta Love the Drunkards

In our daily lives we often come across the sad situation of the person who drinks too much. It is particularly sad when they start way too early in the day. Home improvement salespeople get to visit people on their terms, in their homes. The homeowner who is drunk early in the day seems to be either retired or unemployed. It is often very difficult to notice just how drunk someone is until you have been with them for several minutes.

The other challenge with these people is that it is hard to determine if they are drunk or just normally obnoxious. In Kingston, Tennessee, a contractor was visiting a customer because he had a service issue with his newly installed windows. The problem was not his windows, but the ever pesky, ladybug. This homeowner had ladybugs accumulating on the inside of his windows, and he thought their presence was the result of poorly made windows.

The reality of ladybugs is they can come into a home through many different ways and then they migrate to the windows, wanting out! Now, there is no window company we know of that guarantees your home will be bug free after you install their windows. Trying to communicate this fact to a drunk is hard to do, especially, when they are taking a pee off their back deck.

That's right, this man was trying to argue that the windows are faulty because bugs are in his house while he is taking a pee of his back deck, which is not isolated from his neighbors. The contractor was trying to reason with this man when he walked over to the deck's railing, unzipped his pants, and started peeing off the deck while continuing to argue. How could you take him seriously? He threatened to sue and complain, but the contractor ignored his ramblings and told him there was no warranty to cover bugs entering the home.

The contractor excused himself, and the homeowner was never heard from again. Maybe he totally forgot his point of contention the next day, or his lawyer explained to him that he had no legal ground to stand on, but anyway, he and his bug problem went away. Question: Was that normal behavior or a drunk just being drunk?

On another appointment, Roger was trying to sell windows, and the potential customer kept repeating himself and asking Roger to go back over the same information again. Roger began to suspect the man may be a little too drunk to have all his faculties about him. It was only mid-afternoon though, so he kept moving forward with his presentation until he eventually made the sale.

Roger gladly went over things very slowly, and because the man seemed to understand what was going on, he sold the window replacement project. He was not going to be surprised if the contract cancelled, but he felt the homeowner knew what he was committing to, so the sale was finalized. After Roger made the sale and left copies for the homeowner, he started walking to the steps going down to the front door. The homeowner kept talking to Roger and followed him over to the top of the stairs.

Roger went down the seven or so stairs, said good-bye, then went out the door. As soon as he shut the door, he heard several loud thumping noises, a couple of cuss words, and a bang against the front door. Apparently, the homeowner had fallen down the stairs and into the front door. Roger listened for some sign that the man was still alive, and after hearing a couple more cuss words, he decided to go ahead and leave. The job did not cancel and did get built. Drunks are sadly always entertaining.

U-R-INE IT NOW!

During Halloween, we often see cute little kitty cats depicted as evil, spell-casting satanic drones. Why do we think of these soft balls of fur as the spawn of Satan? Maybe, it is because they scare the crap out of people, look scary at night, or maybe they are just plain and simply bad luck.

Jody, who was mentioned of couple of times already, was a very seasoned tinman, or in more modern terms, a vinyl siding salesman. Because of his great success over the years, he had moved up into management and had the privilege of going on sales calls to observe and coach newer sales reps. One day, Jody went on a presentation and immediately noticed the distinct scent of cat urine while in the home. How homeowners never notice this, we do not know, but there are many homeowners who have no clue that their house stinks. The worse smell is human urine, but cat whiz is right up there.

During this particular visit, Jody sat on the couch while the younger sales rep sat at the dining room table with the homeowner, a single woman in her late 60's. After about ten minutes into the presentation, aside from becoming somewhat nauseous, Jody began to feel a little wet in his pants. At first, he thought something had been spilled on the couch and he was unfortunately providing the service of a paper towel. After another few minutes, Jody noticed there were many cat hairs on the couch, particularly where he was sitting.

Oh, those evil cats! Could this somehow be their sleeping area or their supposed litter box? Jody knew he could not interrupt the sales presentation, so he sat there like the professional he was and literally soaked it all up. After nearly two hours, it was time to leave, and Jody was not hanging around. He smelled like cat pee, was covered in cat hair, and his entire pant bottom was wet and stinky.

Jody held a notepad over his wet pants and quickly excused himself from the home. He and the sales rep got into his car and used a floor mat as a seat cushion because he did not want to get his Cadillac's leather seats wet with cat urine. He had to get home and quickly change. Gotta love the job! Cats can be evil, though.

Who Shall We Fire Today?

Some salesmen always wear a tie and dress slacks to work. This is supposed to make them look more respectable and trustworthy. Unfortunately for some, sales managers get bored during the day while waiting for another appointment, so they think of things to do to avoid getting bored. One idea that came to mind was to go into random retail businesses and start firing people. Because these particular managers and sales reps wore dress shirts and ties, they could actually look like someone of importance in any store.

For this game, the favorite target was the corner drugstore. Here you could find younger employees in a relatively small area who had no idea who they worked for or who signed their paychecks. Tom would go into the stores with his assistant and proceed to the back of the store. With little to no notice, he would tell his assistant that they were going to fire as many people as possible on the way out of the store.

On one such occasion, Tom had his assistant Jeff with him, and they went to the back of the drug store and started looking for an employee who seemed rather new. Jeff carried a clipboard with various papers on it. Tom would walk up to an employee and ask him his name. When he mentioned his name to Tom, he would look to Jeff and ask him if that name was on "the list." Jeff would look at the paper on the clipboard and say it was on the list. Tom would then look at the employee and say, "Did you not get a termination notice with your last paycheck?"

The employee would look quite startled and always say emphatically, "No!" Tom would then start chewing Jeff out for not ensuring the "cut list" was processed with payroll. Jeff would promise Tom it would be in the next pay period, and the two of them would then walk away, leaving the poor employee thinking he was going to be fired.

One day, the two of them fired three people, including a manager, before they left the store. This was done many times throughout central and northern California. They eventually stopped the practice, realizing it was probably not a good thing to do. Of course, as karma goes, Tom was the young boy who actually laid in a street to stop a car and was later run over in Mexico. He was also fired from a job himself later in his career. Again, what goes around comes around.

Why the Chernobyl Nuclear Accident Helped End the Cold War

In nearly any part of the United States, you can drive about forty minutes from a major city in any direction and find those who shouldn't live in a major city. This is why they live outside the city walls, so to speak. I happened to go on an appointment north of Sacramento, California where this was the situation. I did have my assistant sales manager Heidi with me, so we have third party verification that this family does exist.

The home seemed rather inconspicuous at first glance, a one-story, white painted home with a nice porch in front. We pulled up to the home, knocked on the door, and were greeted by a slender gentleman with a full beard. He seemed friendly and welcomed us into his home. We were introduced to his brother, who was apparently the co-owner of the home. He too, was similar in size and general appearance. With the introductions out of the way, we proceeded with the all so important warm-up portion of our sales process.

When we asked them how long they had lived in the home, we somehow got off on a tangent that we had a hard time coming back from. Apparently, this home was purchased by their father and mother, who passed it down to them after they passed away. With the mentioning of their father, the two brothers started boasting about how their dad was a scientist who invented things. I made the fascinating mistake of asking what he had invented. Now, I say mistake because the story that followed was so fascinating that I didn't get them back on topic regarding their siding.

Their father had invented a perpetual motion engine that caused whatever it was in to "float" or move in any direction. Now, that was interesting enough, but apparently the energy field surrounding the engine made it virtually undetectable by modern radar, and it protected whatever it was part of. The first version of this engine was derived from a lawn mower engine. When their father had it ready for testing, after they started the engine, the lawn mower took off straight up from the ground and flew right through the roof. The energy field protected the lawn mower as it went through the roof and into the atmosphere, never to be seen again! The hole in the roof was somehow the same general shape of the lawn mower, including the handle you push the lawnmower with.

With this fascinating discovery, the father contacted some government agencies he knew and shared with them the amazing invention. The US government then set him up in a lab in the State of Nevada for further testing. Eventually, the government helped develop the technology so it could be used on an aircraft. The final product sort of looked round and flat. Yep, they looked like your typical flying saucer.

The government now had a perpetual motion engine that could make aircraft virtually undetectable. As their testing of the technology increased, ideas for different applications were tossed around. During the Cold War years with Russia in the 1980's, tensions were at times rather high, and the threat of military action seemed highly likely. Now, according to the two brothers, President Reagan authorized the use of this technology to scare the Soviet Union into making drastic changes regarding its relationship with the United States.

"What we did is we used this technology to create an undetectable flying aircraft that flew over the Ukraine and hovered above the Chernobyl nuclear facility undetected. We then dropped large bags of concrete onto the nuclear reactor, causing cracks in the facility that resulted in the now infamous Chernobyl nuclear accident of April 1986. This single act scared the Russian government into the realization that the United States had developed a first-strike weapon that was far beyond any known war technology. Russia quickly changed their policies, and soon the Cold War diminished into history. The End". Now you know why I didn't get into much of a sales presentation with these two men. I will leave out the ninja warrior testing they went through for another time.

Dogs and Shoes

Have you ever been asked the question, "Are you interested in a new business opportunity?" Or how about, "What are you doing Wednesday night? Would you like to come over for a little party?" As some of us know, this was a common method of introducing someone to a multi-level marketing business back in the 1980's and 1990's. Do you remember how easy it was to alienate all your friends by trying to help them become rich simply by drawing circles on a dry eraser board?

Maybe this is still going on today, but I haven't been approached for a couple of decades. I guess nobody wants me in his organization. Back in the 1990's, my wife and I were in the thick of it: the events, house parties, and big conferences. Lots of 'Rah 'Rah went with the phrase, "Do you have a dream?!"

I remember one house party back in Sacramento, California, when we helped host a "business opportunity" meeting at one of our recruits' homes. The meeting went well, and this one couple was particularly interested in joining the group. They were a nice, influential couple, and we all had hope of working our business into their big social network that would take us into San Francisco and Los Angeles.

They were successful in their own right and very professional. As is quite customary for many cultures, they took their shoes off before coming into the host's home.

After the meeting, this couple was getting ready to leave, so I walked them to the door to thank them for attending and to confirm our follow-up visit. When we opened the door to look for their shoes, there were no shoes on the front porch. We looked inside and outside but could not find their shoes. After looking for their shoes for several minutes, with no luck in finding them, they walked to their car in their socks. Needless to say, this put them in a very negative and depressed mood. They were probably thinking someone had pulled a practical joke on them or that perhaps this was something even racially motivated. They refused to confirm our follow-up meeting and left quite upset.

The next day, the owners of the home where the meeting was held, called me and said they had found the couple's shoes. They were laying out in the front yard and were not in good shape. Apparently, the host's dogs had gotten out of the backyard during the meeting, went into the front yard, found the shoes and proceeded to have a good time with their new chew toys.

The dogs had totally demolished the shoes, and any hope we had of sponsoring the couple. The homeowners had to pay for the shoes, and they became disenchanted with the whole event and quit the business. Are dogs really man's best friend? Or are they evil too, just like cats?

Quality Hires Make the Best Salespeople

One of the toughest sales positions to have is that of a telemarketer. These poor people have to sit in a small, three-sided cubicle wearing a headset all day, doing nothing but dialing one homeowner after the other. They take the most abusive comments and are often hung-up on—with prejudice. Phones are slammed in their ears, and it is quite normal to receive a few cuss words.

Now, finding someone to sit down and take this kind of abuse is not easy. I must say, though, there are some who adapt to this environment and do make some pretty decent money. There is a company ladder to climb into management, and business owners will pay good money for an appointment. At one company where I worked, each home improvement appointment cost about three hundred to four hundred dollars—whether it is sold or not! Our reps would often visit two or three appointments in one day.

At one company, the pressure to produce appointments was getting rather heavy on a management team, so they decided to hire some applicants before they finished a full background check on each.

This one young lady had passed her drug test and said on her application that she had never been convicted of a felony. So why not get her started?

Well, after about a week of employment, the background check came back stating that this person had been convicted of a felony. Not just any felony, though. We are talking murder. Yep, apparently she *and her family* were convicted of murder and sentenced to many years in prison. This young lady was released before her family (including her mother) because she was just an accessory. You know, like a good piece of jewelry.

The question I had to ask as I watched her being politely and apologetically escorted out the front door was, "What kind of family did she have?" The story was that her family killed another family. Family-on-family crime! Sounds like the old Hatfields and McCoys. They say there are crazy people living in California. Well, that was a new one for me.

Lights Out, Knock Out

Sometimes sales reps react to situations instead of thinking first. One time, Clark was training a new sales rep, and the potential customer was a woman named Cindy, who had a strong belief in palm reading and the religious gift of healing. During the sales presentation, Cindy told Clark she would like to read his palm. Clark stated he was an open book, and what you see is what you get, but this guy (pointing to the person with him) was somewhat of a mystery, so maybe she should read his palm.

Cindy then took the sales rep's palm and began to massage and stare at his hand. While she was looking at his hand, she said he was holding in lots of frustration and anger. She said she could help him release those negative feelings. She then began to hum some indistinguishable words and then she suddenly slapped him in the forehead with the palm of her hand. As soon as she slapped him in the head, he punched her in the face. She fell to the floor, knocked out like a boxer who had taken a punch from a heavyweight champion. Unfortunately, his natural reaction to being slapped in the head was to punch the aggressor. Apparently, he had some real latent frustration issues with a low tolerance threshold for surprises. Oh, by the way, she was out cold on the floor for only a second or two.

Clark was absolutely floored by the situation. He asked aloud, "Is she dead?" Both men stared at the poor woman lying on the floor and were dumbfounded. Fortunately, Cindy came to quickly and sat up on the floor saying, "I guess I shouldn't have slapped you in the head!" The two men helped her up, back onto her chair, and offered their apologies.

Clark was thinking she might call the police, or even file a lawsuit. He also thought they could be fired from the company. After she regained her senses, she asked them to continue with their presentation, which they did. The funny thing is, they did make a sale! No charges were ever filed, and nobody learned of the incident at work. Both men kept their jobs, and another unbelievable story was kept secret for a few months—just to make sure they were in the clear. As the old saying goes, "If they don't buy, punch them in the face until they do." (Sales tactic #110.)

Bad Driver Defense

Another challenge salespeople have is the interaction with all of the slow, stupid drivers who drive slowly in the fast lane or drive fast to get by you and then pull directly in front of you, taking away the safe driving distance you had before they pulled in front of you. Outside salespeople sometimes travel over forty thousand miles per year and usually become some of the best drivers on the highways. However, driving defensively is a critical skill-set to have in order to stay safe. Being aware of one's surroundings and keeping an eye out for reckless drivers is important to any driver. The old saying, "You can't fix stupid," is also important to remember. Otherwise, you can become full of road rage.

Some of the drivers we encounter cannot help themselves from endangering the lives of others. They are just stupid. One of the anti-stupidity tactics we developed was the use of a cell phone and a sheriff's hat. Many cell phones have a screen that looks a little blue or red in color when in use. What we did to make stupid drivers move out of the way when we needed to get by them was to take our cell phones, and while the screen is lit up, spin it around and around on top of the dash, creating the image of a flashing authority vehicle. When the driver in front of you looks in his rearview mirror and sees that small light rotating around and around, he often pulls into the right lane and lets you go by. If you were late for an evening appointment during the winter, this was very helpful.

Now, if you were also wearing a hat that had "Sheriff" printed on the front in nice raised letters, the driver would hit his brakes and drop his speed way down. As you drove by, he would often give you "the nod." You know, the nod of respect. It is amazing how effective these techniques are in clearing the lane in front of you! I would sometimes just set the sheriff hat on the dash with the lettering facing forward. You could see people look in their rearview mirrors, then quickly pull over and let you go by. Again, you would get the nod.

Also, if you see someone texting, you can pull up next to him with your sheriff's hat on and stare at him for a second or two. When he sees you looking at him, you simulate with your hands texting on a phone and shake your head. Funny thing is, drivers usually put their phone down, place two hands on the steering wheel, and look straight ahead. The cell phone helps at night and the sheriff hat is mainly for the daytime. Drive safely!

California Nudists

As you are learning from reading these stories, home improvement salespeople meet some of the strangest Americans. While on a siding appointment in California, I met a single, middle-aged lady who was into the vegan lifestyle, yoga, and meditation. She was divorced and a little different but very nice. While we were outside looking at the exterior of her home, I noticed a heavy plastic bag with what appeared to be a shower nozzle on the underside of the bag. Being a little curious, I asked her what it was for, and she said, without any hesitation, "That is my shower bag that I use when I am outside working in my yard." I asked her if she used it to wash her hands and tools. She quickly replied, "Oh, no I am a nudist, so when I work in the yard, I simply take a quick shower outside and dry off before I go inside."

Now, that was a first for me. I immediately began to look at the fence to see just how private her back yard was, and for the most part it was, except for the two-story home behind her. And yes, she was fairly attractive. I didn't sell that one, but if I had, I'll bet the installation crew would have enjoyed working there!

On another visit just southeast of Sacramento, I followed my map to an address that took me to a resort community of some type. There was a small parking lot outside of the entrance, and when looking in, I could see several small shacks or homes with narrow streets between them. Even though this was a little unusual, I parked my car and went through the entrance to what appeared to be an office building.

When inside, I had a hard time finding anyone to talk with, but eventually a woman appeared and asked if she could help me. I mentioned to her that I was there for an appointment with a Mr. and Mrs. Jones regarding a home improvement project. She didn't know anyone by that name, so she asked that I sit in this large room with tables and stools while she checked into my inquiry.

As I sat on the stool, I began to look around at the rather large room and noticed some pictures on the walls. These pictures seemed to be of an event that was held in the very room I was sitting in. As I looked closer, it became quite apparent that none of the dozens of people in the photos were wearing any clothes. There were people of all sizes and shapes, young adults, and some that were too old to be nude! I also noticed that they were sitting naked on the same stool that I was sitting on! Ugh! Talk about being grossed out! I immediately went over to a faucet, grabbed a paper towel, used it to turn the faucet on, and then washed my hands.

I did not sit back down in that room again. This was not a resort of normal sorts; it was a full-fledged nudist colony. Fortunately, I think, the lady came back and said the people I was looking for had a home in the resort and it was "over that way." So, hesitantly, off I went to wander through the nudist colony.

As I am going along, I see a pool that looked nice, with unusual surroundings. About half of the sides surrounding the pool were constructed of concrete with a tiered-step design. Starting about ten feet from the edge of the pool, the concrete stepped up about a foot in height, then went into the hill about six feet or so. It then tiered up again, went back about six feet or so, and then continued this pattern for about ten steps.

Now, I had never seen this before, so I stopped and wondered. It then dawned on me. This was designed for the nudists to lay out and tan around the pool. I then pictured in my mind, all of those people I saw in those pictures up in the main office building lying out on the concrete tiers naked. Oh, my gosh! What a sight! Could you imagine flying over in a helicopter or a low flying aircraft and seeing these beached, over-weight, wrinkled people lying out like sea lions on a beach! Wow!

Fortunately for me, there was nobody home at the location, so I was off the hook on this one. Gotta love the California nudist societies!

Department Store Humor

Having a good assistant doesn't always mean she is good just because of a skill related to her job. It can mean she "gets you," and the two of you can work together effectively and have fun. To me, having good co-workers and assistants means they are good at their jobs, and together we can help keep the daily grind enjoyable. I had a great assistant named Heidi, who was someone I could depend on and trust.

While working one day, we had some time between appointments, so we stopped into a very large and popular department store. I wanted to buy a new dress shirt, so we planned that she would "assist" me by being the one who communicated with any store associate who wanted to help me. As we started looking at shirts, a store associate came up to me and politely asked if she could help me find anything. Instead of answering her, I leaned over to Heidi and whispered into her ear what I wanted.

Heidi in turn began to explain what I was looking for, saying, "We are looking for a dark blue dress shirt, seventeen and a half inch neck with thirty-four inch arms. Preferably something that doesn't wrinkle easily." Of course, this was done with a straight face by Heidi.

The expression on the store associate's face was priceless. Sure enough, all conversations went through my assistant from then on. I ended up sitting down in a chair, and Heidi brought the shirts to me to consider. At times I would get a look of disgust or disbelief on my face, then gesture to her to take the shirt back. This continued until I found the right shirt. The fun part was, when we paid for it, I gave the money to Heidi, and she conducted the transaction for me.

That associate just stared at us as we left her department. I am sure she shared that story with her store co-workers and family when she got home. We, of course, just laughed and congratulated each other on another fun adventure.

Not to try to outdo ourselves, we did go into another large, upper-end department store on another day. It was apparently their anniversary because they had large number of store associates helping and offering free samples of this and that. We were approached by a nice young female associate who asked if we would like to try a new hand lotion.

Heidi and I simply looked at each other and smiled. We knew it was a golden opportunity for another humorous interaction. You see, we were doing reality TV shows before they became popular. With this setup, I took the lead and looked at the store associate and asked her if this was a body cream and not just a hand cream. She said it could be used anywhere. So I looked at Heidi, then looked back at the associate, and asked, "Could you please put it all over my body?" I did not smile or stutter. This was done in a very polite manner and with all sincerity. She looked and me said, "Excuse me?"

At this point, I looked to Heidi and gestured to her with my hands, beckoning her to intercede for me. Heidi was a natural, and with a calm manner, she picked up the conversation. "He would like you to put the cream on his entire body." The store associate was stunned. She smiled and asked one more time what we meant. I whispered into Heidi's ear, and she in turn mentioned to the associate that we could use a changing room if that would be more comfortable for her. With her eyes wide open, she said, "Sorry, but I cannot help you with that request."

I nicely shrugged my shoulders and said, "I guess we will have to pass on the cream. Thank you." As we walked away, Heidi looked back, and the associate was still looking at us, shaking her head in disbelief as to what just happened. Just another casual day for us!

QUALITY CRAFTSMEN

In the home improvement industry, one of the biggest challenges of recruiting good, dependable installation crews is finding someone who can pass a background check and a drug test. One of my peers, John, from Chattanooga, Tennessee, shared with me that he held a free breakfast at a local hotel and advertised that he was looking for installation crews.

When you offer a free breakfast, you will get all types and literally dozens of "contractors." The registration of attendees indicated over seventy people came to this free breakfast. My friend John was very excited about the possibility of fulfilling his installation needs. After about a half hour or so of mingling and eating, he gathered the potential recruits together and first thanked them for coming. He then mentioned that to work for his company, every contractor and person working for that contractor would have to successfully pass a background check and drug test. He also mentioned that they would have to have a valid driver's license and carry liability insurance.

As soon as he made this announcement, he paused and watched about fifty-plus people leave the room. He ended up with about fifteen to twenty people still in the room, probably thinking they would be able to pass the stringent requirements. These types of results are not uncommon. Even if they pass the tests and checks, you then had to worry about their knowledge of social etiquette, being well-mannered, and simply having some common sense.

In Colorado, we had carefully hired a siding installation crew and vetted them the best we could. Despite our best efforts, we received a call from our customer who was in the middle of her week-long installation. She started the conversation as many do, stating that she didn't want to get someone fired, *but*. The story then continued with her stating that she and her seven year-old daughter were home eating a nice breakfast, and her daughter asked her mother, "Mommy, what is that man doing out behind our bushes?"

As she described the scenario, she started with how they live in a nice, middle-class neighborhood. Lots of children and families were living in her subdivision. Most backyards do not have any fences, so everyone can see what goes on in their neighbors' backyards.

With that being said, she then shared how she and her daughter looked out in the backyard, and while looking at a hedgerow, they could see a man's bare legs, with his pants down to his ankles, pooping in the grass. Yep, he dumped a load in their backyard while the mother and her young daughter watched.

They didn't say a word to him, but they called our company promptly. What can you say in this situation? Sometimes, there are not enough words to say that could possibly make things better. With this incident, you just take the customer's feedback, swallow any portion of pride you had in your company, and offer them a large financial discount for their troubles.

Even the salespeople do some rather dumb things when it comes to social grace. I had a salesperson who had passed all the checks and tests and was an existing hire when I started managing for a new company. This rep's name was Joe, and he had once been in the rodeo circuit and to some degree fancied himself to be a cowboy. Word was that he did fairly well when working the rodeo circuit, but he got in some type of accident that busted up his skull pretty bad. He had to find another profession, and it was selling home improvements.

Now, he is a very nice person and normally quite polite and considerate. Maybe this day was just an off day. Or maybe the head injury may have impacted some insight and self-awareness. Who knows why this happened, but here is what he did. One time, while trying to sell a new kitchen remodel to a lady, he decided to spit in her kitchen sink while he was trying to "evaluate" her existing cabinets' condition. As soon as he spit his slimy tobacco juice into her sink, her jaw dropped, and she asked him, "Did you just spit into my sink?"

Joe, without hesitation, quickly replied, "I sure did. Is that okay?" The homeowner was absolutely dumbfounded. She asked him why he would do that, and he simply said, "That is what I do at my house." At this point, she was "over" Joe and abruptly asked him to leave. Needless to say, as the manager of the rep, I am the one who received the phone call and the complaint. What do you say? All I could say is, "I am sorry and we will take corrective action to ensure Joe never does this type of thing again."

The Stockton, CA Avenues

Every town has a neighborhood or two that you need to be very careful around when visiting. For some reason, in Stockton, California, many of the low-numbered avenue streets seem to have this common persona. On one appointment in the Avenues, we were having a hard time finding a home. The house numbers were often not on the homes, so we would have to resort to either driving slowly up and down the street or to parking and walking up and down the street asking random people if they knew the particular house number we were looking for.

When you are in some of the tougher neighborhoods, driving slowly up and down the street is not a good idea. Walking up and down may not be better, but I guess you can pick your poison. In this neighborhood, we decided to get out of the car and try to find the home on foot.

While standing on the sidewalk looking for the house number on one home, we noticed a grungy-looking man, maybe in his early twenties, coming down the sidewalk in our direction. He stopped, looked at us, and turned away. It seemed he had changed his mind and was going to walk the other way. We have had young kids in these neighborhoods ask us if we were cops or the CIA before, so maybe he thought that the two guys in ties were people to avoid.

I was about to turn away from his direction when I noticed he stopped, stared at the sidewalk for a second, then turned back around and began walking toward us quite rapidly. When he was about two houses away, he reached into the back of his pants and pulled out what looked like a large Bowie knife. Some may have called it a Rambo knife. What the heck was this guy going to do?

I pointed this man out to the new rep I was training and said to him, "We might want to get into the car." As we were starting to move toward our car, the guy stopped, looked at us, and then with great intensity, he yelled and stabbed a garbage can that was in the street for pickup. He stabbed the can twice, looked at us again, then turned and walked away. He went to the end of the block, turned the corner, and we never saw him again. What was that all about?

While on another Stockton appointment, we somehow ended up driving on a dirt road that was actually in town. The neighborhood seemed rather seedy. Of course, there were no house numbers that you could read, and the street signs were few and far between. Our GPS was helpful, but finding the appointment required us to slow down and look hard.

While driving past one house, we saw a sign in the yard. This was a homemade wood sign with verbiage that had been painted on it with red paint. The words were a first for me: "Do not pick up or drop off your whores here." Now, that is a good indication you may be in a dangerous neighborhood.

To continue the story, we found our address, knocked on the door, and an old-looking young lady answered the door and informed us we were at the right home, but her mom was at work. Old-looking young lady, you ask? Well, she looked about 40 or so, but there were indications she was only in her twenties. The scars and scabs on her arms and the wrinkles in her face and around her dark eyes made her look older. The needle track marks up her arm may have indicated some serious drug usage. For the most part, she was friendly to the two of us and asked for us to come in and wait for her mom.

We passed on the invitation, as tempting as she was, and decided to leave as soon as we could. The next time a lead came across my desk for that neighborhood, I gave it to one of the sales reps who was on my crap list.

Sorry to Hear That

For the true exterior home improvement salesperson, the first basic achievement you need to accomplish in order to be respected among your peers is to one-call close your first sale over twenty thousand dollars and to make a sale at an appointment at eight o'clock in the evening. We used to enjoy sending new salespeople out into the countryside during the winter months on late evening visits. They were either in or out after a few of those.

If I could, I would make sure the appointment was about an hour and a half from our office, in the opposite direction of his home. Some called it hazing; we called it training. It was not unusual, though, for a few of the weaker ones to quit after these "training" appointments. Now, if they sold one, we gave them the nod and treated them like they were part of the team. If they didn't, well, let's just say their armor had a dent in it and the hazing continued. We were a tight group, once you were "made."

One of the better sales reps I ever worked with was Jeff. He did anything he was asked and did it reasonably well. I would say he was an exceptional home improvement salesperson. He took the late-night appointments without complaining and could sell quite well.

A common routine for the veteran reps in our office was to call each other on the way home from the evening appointments. We enjoyed talking with each other and sharing all of these weird stories. We normally sold our evening appointments. Anyone who would set an appointment at eight o'clock at night was serious about their project.

After one such appointment, Jeff called right when he left a home and was reviewing how his appointment went. For some reason, he had to reset his meeting with the homeowners for the following evening. I do not remember why, but he was going to go back at eight o'clock the following night. Now, this was a really good appointment because they set it twice for eight o'clock, so Jeff was excited about the opportunity.

While Jeff was talking with me on the phone, I heard this thumping sound through the phone. It sounded as if he had hit something. He stopped his car, got out to look around, but didn't see any damage, so he got back in and drove off. When he got home later that evening, he looked at his car a little closer, and when looking at a front wheel, he found remnants of what used to be a cat.

Now, Jeff was not a big cat lover, so he called me immediately to share what had happened. For some reason, I could see him smiling while he discussed the horrific scene. Cat hair and skin were all over his wheel well. While he was talking about the incident, he stopped in the middle of his thoughts and said, "You know what, the people I was visiting tonight had a couple of cats. I wonder if this was one of theirs?"

Now, we both thought the idea of Jeff not making a sale, having to reset for the next evening, and then killing their cat when leaving was a little weird. We were now curious how his "be-back" appointment would go the next evening. Sure enough, when he went back and started with some casual warm-up conversation, they shared that they were quite sad because one of their family cats was hit and killed the night before.

I do not know how Jeff kept a straight face, but he followed the basic principles of Selling 101 and immediately empathized with their situation, acted like he cared (but remember, he hates cats), and then proceeded to sell them vinyl siding for their home. Yep, he acted like he knew nothing about the accident, shared in their sorrow, and made about a thousand dollars commission—after killing their cat!

Jeff's comments when they told him about the cat were, "Really, that is too bad. Sorry to hear that!" Don't say he was horrible. What would you have done?

Auditions Anyone?

In between another set of appointments in Davis, California, a couple of seasoned sales reps were feeling a little rambunctious because neither one had made a sale that morning. With lunchtime upon them, they decided to stop by a local fast food burger joint and grab some grub. They must have missed the main lunch crowd because there was hardly anyone in the place.

Among many organizations there is often a rite of passage for newer members, and the same is often true within home improvement sales teams. As usual, Tom and Jeff were a little bored, so they called a newer sales rep who was working in the same area and asked him to come over and join them for lunch.

Gene arrived and was excited that the two senior veterans had invited him to lunch. After getting their lunch down, Jeff and Tom asked Gene if he would like to make some extra money. Gene said of course, so Tom made up a challenge for him.

"I will give you ten dollars if you stand on top of this table and start dancing," Tom offered. Gene said, "No way, not for only ten dollars!"

"Well, how about for twenty dollars?" replied Tom.

"How long do I have to dance?"

"About thirty seconds, and you have to really shake it!"

After some hesitation, young Gene jumped up on the table and started dancing.

Jeff and Tom started laughing, and by the way, the place was not empty of patrons. When people started looking, Tom stated that they were auditioning for a movie and wanted to check out the spontaneous ability of Gene for a comedy role. This was California, so the diners actually bought the idea.

It did help that Jeff and Tom were wearing dress shirts and ties, so they looked somewhat official for being in a burger joint. Fortunately, there was a wall blocking the view of the employees, so they did not know what everyone was laughing about. Gene finished his role, collected his twenty dollars, and wiped down the table with some damp napkins, and they all went off to work. Just another day at work for this sales team.

Conclusion

I hope you can now understand why some of us really enjoy the world of sales. If you can have fun while you work, then I think you have it made. Best wishes and I hope you have some stories to share yourself someday. Thank you for reading Sales Tales! I greatly appreciate my coworkers who have shared their stories with me over the years and my family who put up with the weird hours I worked. Hopefully, you will read Sales Tales Too when it comes out.